Beer and
Skittles

Richard Boston was born in 1938. After two years
as an art student in London, he went to King's
College, Cambridge, where he read English. At
various times he has taught in Sicily, Sweden, France
and the University of London, and pursued an
extremely brief acting career which resulted in
fleeting appearances in Jacques Tati's *Playtime*. He
has worked on the staff of *The Times Literary Supplement*
and *New Society*, appears regularly on radio and television, and has written widely for newspapers and
magazines in Britain and the United States. In
1973 he began to contribute a regular weekly
column to the *Guardian* on all aspects of beer. His
first book, *An Anatomy of Laughter*, was published in
1974, and *The Admirable Urquhart*, his edition of the
writings of Sir Thomas Urquhart, appeared in 1975.

D1374055

Beer and Skittles

RICHARD BOSTON

Fontana/Collins

First published by William Collins Sons & Co. Ltd
Glasgow 1976
First issued in Fontana 1977

Made and printed in Great Britain by
William Collins Sons & Co. Ltd Glasgow

Contents

Acknowledgements

Parts of this book originally appeared in slightly different form in the *Guardian*: I am grateful to the editor for permission to recycle the material. Many thanks also to Mrs Elizabeth David for many helpful comments and suggestions about beer in cooking; to Gordon Bailey and Christopher Hyde of Hydes' Brewery; to Peter Evans and David Smith of the Brewers' Society; to Ben Davis, for pointing out to me much about pub design that I would not have noticed for myself; for information, assistance, advice, criticism and encouragement to Anne Boston, Frank Baillie, Jo Foster, Alicia Freundlich, Michael Hardman, Christopher Hutt, Harold Jackson, C. O. Jones, Michael McNay, Derek Peebles, Arthur Taylor, William Tayleur, Keith Walker, Ken Wortelhock, Philip Ziegler, and especially to Rod Prince; to Greene, King and Sons for permission to reproduce the chart on page 52; to the readers of the *Guardian*, without whom this book would never have been started; and to Jack and Heather Macaulay, Harold and Pearl Newbery, and Graham and Pat Watts, who have served me many excellent pints without which this book would have been finished much sooner, but less enjoyably.

Hermit hoar, in solemn cell,
Wearing out life's evening gray;
Strike thy bosom, Sage! and tell
What is bliss, and which the way?
Thus I spoke, and speaking sigh'd,
Scarce repress'd the starting tear,
When the hoary Sage reply'd,
"Come, my lad, and drink some beer."

Samuel Johnson

I Good Things

When I was almost fifteen my elder brother took me to a pub. This made me feel very bold, and I could hardly refuse the even more grown-up offer of half a pint. I'd had bottled beer at home, but never draught bitter. The first sip was horrific. I vividly remember the shiver that went down my spine at the appalling bitterness of the stuff, and the dismay with which I registered the sheer quantity that was half a pint. We were somewhere near Westerham at the time, so it was probably a Fremlin's pub, or else Westerham Ales (which no longer exists). In any case it was probably strongly hopped, as was usual in the hop-growing county of Kent. Somehow I got through that half, but I'm sure I didn't have any more that day. Over the next year or two the experience was repeated and I came to tolerate and then actually enjoy the taste.

This must be a fairly common experience. In *A Sort of Life* Graham Greene describes his first taste of beer:

> I was offered beer first by Lubbock, my riding master, whom I visited one evening in summer. I hated the taste and drank it down with an effort to prove my manliness, and yet some days later, on a long country walk with Raymond, the memory of the taste came back to taunt my thirst. We stopped at an inn for bread and cheese, and I drank bitter for the second time and enjoyed the taste with a pleasure that has never failed me since.

I have no idea who brewed any of the beer I drank in the years immediately before, during and after my time at university, with the single exception of an especially delicious pint of draught Bass in a pub somewhere underground near Charing Cross station. In those days one chose a pub more or less at random and simply asked for bitter. I did, however, have a friend I considered unduly fussy who used to make a point of avoiding Watney's pubs.

Cambridge and a couple of years knocking about in London was followed by a spell abroad in Sweden and France. In Paris the drink was naturally wine. It's the best in the world and at that time was cheap, whereas the beer was expensive and in the case of the *pression* (draught) tasted of metal polish. By the time I returned to England in the mid-1960s I was looking forward to getting back to English beer – only to find that I didn't like it. I attributed my disappointment to a change in taste caused by a year in Paris, and accordingly drank wine and spirits and sometimes, without much pleasure, beer. Looking back I can remember two experiences which should have shown that it was not me that had changed but the beer. Some time around 1965 I went for a holiday which took me by train through Germany, Czechoslovakia and Austria. This was before Dubcek's time, and Novotny's Prague must have been a tough place to live in. To me it seemed delightful. The setting of the city was magnificent, the architecture grand without being intimidating; the eye was not constantly assaulted by advertisements, nor the lungs, ears and human life itself endangered by roaring, polluting automobiles. The food was stodgy, low in taste and protein, but my God the beer was good. I had only intended to stay in Prague for two days: I knew no one there, I hadn't much money and there was little to do. I stayed nearly a week, going from place to place drinking this wonderful beer and feeling more and more like the good soldier Svejk.

At least I liked Czech beer. I liked some English beer too, for it must have been around the same time that my brother, who had emigrated to Australia, returned home for the first time in five years. One evening we took my mother out from Whitstable, where she was living, to a place we had spotted in the *Good Food Guide*. It was a pub

called the Red Lion at Wingham, and before the meal we
had some beer. Ten years is a long time, memory blurs
and taste changes, but I would still say that it was the best
beer I've ever drunk. At a time when I thought I didn't
like English beer, I liked it. My brother, who had come back
making unfavourable comparisons between English beer
and Australian, liked it. My mother, who probably drinks
as much beer in ten years as a Sheffield steel-worker in a
weekend, liked it. We had intended to have wine with the
meal, but all agreed to go on as we had started. It was the
very poetry of beer.

Later I learnt that it was brewed by Gardner's of Ash,
which supplied only two or three pubs. Shortly afterwards
Gardner's was taken over by Tomson and Wotton, which
was in turn swallowed by Whitbread's. The Red Lion now
serves Whitbread Trophy.

If the Czech experience had shown me I still liked beer,
the Gardner's one should have shown me that I still liked
English beer, though not what was in most of the pubs in
London. I now realize that the reason I went off beer in
general in the mid-1960s was that without my knowing it
I was drinking something different. By merely asking for
bitter, or mouthing a name I had seen in television advertisements, I was getting something sweet and gassy which
I didn't like – in short, keg beer. A friend once tried to
explain it all to me, but it seemed rather technical: besides,
I was growing to like bottled Guinness.

In 1972, while suffering from a severe cash-flow crisis, I
undertook some hack-work for an American firm on a guide
to London pubs. The book never appeared, but going
round a number of pubs was an educational experience.
First I was appalled by what the brewers had done to pubs
I hadn't visited for years: then I gradually began to realize
what they had done to the beer. The familiar hand pumps
were rapidly vanishing, being replaced by top-pressure CO_2
systems that made the beer fizzy. Even worse, the traditional

draught beer (in whatever way it was served) was becoming hard to find and the much-advertised, gaudily-presented keg beers were being vigorously promoted.

There was still good beer to be found, even in London, but you had to look for it. In central London most of it was in Bass Charrington pubs, where real beer was often still delivered by hand pumps. Further out were the Young's pubs, mostly in the Wandsworth area, and Fuller, Smith and Turner's over at Chiswick. These independent breweries showed that not all beer tastes the same.

I awoke to what was happening to English beer at about the same time as many other people. The idea of writing a beer column started in a fairly jokey kind of way. A reader had written to the *Guardian* pointing out that there were plenty of wine correspondents about but no one to lead the beer drinker through the thickets. I talked about it with Michael McNay and Harold Jackson of the *Guardian* and we agreed it was a good idea. One could have a go at the big brewers; one could point to the surviving local brewers of traditional beer; there was pub architecture; pub games, pubs in literature – oh yes, there was material for several weeks at least. Accordingly in the summer of 1973 I started writing a weekly column, appearing on Saturdays, on beer, pubs and allied topics.

It quickly became apparent that the idea interested far more people than we had expected. Letters poured in, full of suggestions, information, appreciation and encouragement. I take no particular credit for the fact that 'Boston on Beer', as the column came to be called, acted as something of a catalyst. The same would have happened if the column had been much better or much worse. By a chance that for me was a happy one, there was nothing else like it anywhere around. Thanks to the *Guardian* and its readers I was able to collect and pass on information about breweries that were still producing traditional beer (mostly the surviving independent regional breweries), to attack what the big companies were doing to beer and pubs, and generally to write about the subject in a way appropriate to what is after all a major part of the nation's leisure activities.

Teasing and baiting the big breweries was great fun, but what was also needed if they were to be made to feel the weight of the consumers' demands was some kind of organized body, and this was provided with skill and some panache by Camra (the Campaign for Real Ale).

I think that three years ago the most anyone hoped for was that our protests and derision might, even if only ever so slightly, slow down what the big bad brewers were doing to beer and pubs. Within two years it was apparent not only that this was happening but also that the brewers were actually changing tack and reversing previous policies. The consumer revolt against the big brewers that has taken place in the past three or four years is unique. I know of no other industry of this size that has been checked in the direction it had taken by the massive resistance of the customers. This is gratifying to beer drinkers, but the achievement is one that is important to others as well. It has demonstrated that we need not be endlessly manipulated by the forces of the state or big business.

We should be able to take the simple things for granted. It is ridiculous that we have to seek out a good loaf of bread as though hunting for a gastronomic luxury, but it's no exaggeration to say that in some parts of the country good bread is as rare as truffles. Unless you can find a health food shop or one of the diminishing number of one-man bakeries you're almost certain to find yourself with pre-sliced bread wrapped in waxed paper: it is never really fresh but it takes a long time to go stale (it usually goes mouldy first); it's expensive, has no taste, and on being eaten forms a wodge like a clenched fist high up in the chest where it can cause acute discomfort for hours.

The sausage is increasingly a standardized product, low in flavour and dubious in contents. As Jane Grigson says (in her book from which I have borrowed the title of this chapter), 'It is easier to put no seasoning to speak of into a sausage – it offends nobody, everybody buys it. This is the theory. We're back to the primitive idea of eating to keep alive.'

Eggs are pale in shell and yolk, and are laid by hens in concentration camps. Kippers are dyed and packed in plastic: the real thing is almost unobtainable. Instead of those wrinkled, scarred, funny-shaped green-and-red delicious tomatoes you get in Italy, we are sold tomatoes that are perfectly red, perfectly round and almost perfectly tasteless.

What all these things have in common is blandness, an absence of character. They're not sweet and they're not sour, they're not stale and they're not fresh. They are offensive for their inoffensiveness, like the Laodiceans denounced by St John the Divine in *Revelation*: 'I know thy works, that thou are neither cold nor hot: I would thou wert cold or hot. So then because thou art lukewarm, and neither cold nor hot, I will spue thee out of my mouth.'

Today you have to go out of your way to find real bread, or Cheddar cheese with a rind on, or fresh chickens, or eggs from free-range hens. The battle for these things was lost without a shot being fired. This resulted partly from a shameful indifference on the part of the consumer, partly from defeatism. Standardized, mass-produced and extremely expensive convenience foods have replaced varied, and variable, local produce. The reasons why the major brewers were keen to replace traditional beer with what is called keg beer will be explained later. Here it is sufficient to say that keg beer is a Laodicean product in every respect except that it is not lukewarm: usually it is served rather cold, in order to disguise its lack of taste. Its character, however, is utterly lukewarm. Whereas real beer can be very good or very bad, keg is consistently mediocre. It is an exaggeration to say that much-promoted drinks like Watney's Red, Allied's Double Diamond, Courage's Tavern, Younger's Tartan, Whitbread's Tankard and keg Worthington E are revolting. The exaggeration is pardonable but it is still an exaggeration. They don't actually make your gorge rise, which the very worst of real beer could conceivably do. But they are sweet and gassy, like Coca-Cola and all sorts of mineral waters which I don't personally like but which I can drink without vomiting. What I want when I ask for a pint of bitter is something quite different, a beer that is fairly flat in appearance, that is served at about room temperature, that smacks of hops and tastes bitter.

Unlike the consumers of bread and cheese, beer drinkers woke up in time to protest successfully against standardization. By the beginning of 1975 I began to feel that so far as my *Guardian* column was concerned, I could let up a little. The information had been put across, in so far as it was ever going to be, and the polemical points had been made. Accordingly the column ceased to be exclusively about beer and pubs, and turned to other matters while continuing to make frequent trips to Publand. That inexhaustibly fascinating country is the subject of this book. In spite of the worst the big brewers have been able to do, there is still fine English beer, and there are still fine English pubs. Though there is much to criticize, there is still more to celebrate.

II   4000 B.C. and All That

Various kinds of fruit are instant do-it-yourself wine kits, complete with their own sugar and even, in the bloom on the skin, their own yeast. All you have to do with grapes, for example, is crush them and they will ferment into a drinkable form of alcohol. Making beer is much more difficult, since the barley has first to be turned into malt. This is a sophisticated technique requiring considerable skill, but it was one that was known in the Middle East some 4,000 or more years BC. Ale was so popular that according to the Greeks Dionysus (Bacchus) fled from Mesopotamia in disgust at the people's addiction to the drink. In Sumer nearly half the total grain yield was used in brewing, an activity that was carried out under the protecting eye of Ninkasi, a goddess who also looked after baking. The association of brewing and baking suggests a possible explanation of how the malting process was discovered. The neolithic baker used sprouted grains to make flour, and it was found that bread made from this flour kept better. According to Reay Tannahill (*Food in History*), in the early Egyptian period a dough was made from sprouted, dried grains and then partly baked. The loaves were then broken up and soaked, and after a day's fermenting the liquor was strained off and ready to drink. The result must have been fairly revolting, and certainly gave rise to widespread complaints, as indeed beer has ever since. Graffiti discovered by archaeologists in Ur of the Chaldees show that the inhabitants thought that the quality of the drink had deteriorated, and the first legal code ever devised, that of King Hammurabi of Babylon in about 1750 BC, condemned weak and over-priced ale.

The Egyptians may have been slightly more fortunate. They were taught how to brew by Osiris, and had a kind of beer called *zythum*. This is the last word in Chambers Dictionary and was highly praised by Diodorus.

An intriguing detail about the habits of these pioneering pubmen and women is that, at least in Mesopotamia, representations of beer-drinkers invariably show them drinking through straws. Some scholars consider that this was to prevent the hulls of the malted barley getting into the drinker's mouth. This is unlikely, since Mesopotamian technology could easily have come up with a strainer. It seems more probable that it was a sociable act, rather like passing a mug around, since most of the pictures show two or more Mesopotamians sucking from a single receptacle. (Philip Ziegler tells me that the Meos of South-East Asia still drink their rice wine from a communal pot through straws.) Another explanation may simply be that, as children know, drinking through straws is fun. Even so, it never really caught on as a way of drinking and went out completely for four or five thousand years, only to be revived quite recently by a little old lady I observed in a public bar in Lancaster in March 1974. She was sitting quietly in a corner drinking a bottle of Guinness through a straw. Apparently this was her regular practice.

The Celts of the Iron Age in Britain drank a kind of ale called *curmi*, a name which survives in Welsh *cwrw* and Irish *cuirn*. Mead, however, was the main native-produced alcoholic drink, and when the Romans arrived they brought quantities of wine with them. By King Alfred's time ale was well-established, and he listed it among the requirements of the men he needed to run the country – 'land to live on, and gifts and weapons, and ale and food and clothes' (quoted by H. A. Monckton in his useful *A History of Ale and Beer*). Alehouses were common in Anglo-Saxon England, and by the time of Edward the Confessor ale was considered good enough to be the chief drink at a banquet.

Most ale at this time would have been home-brewed, but the Domesday Book mentions 43 brewers (*cerevisiarii*) and shows that the maintenance of standards by public brewers was, as so often throughout history, a matter of concern. In Chester the penalty for brewing bad ale (*malam cerevisiam faciens*) was punishment by ducking or a fine of four shillings.

Though the ruling Normans and Plantaganets were wine-drinkers, English ale was thought of sufficiently highly for Thomas à Becket to take a considerable quantity with him when he went to France on a diplomatic mission in 1158. Two chariots were laden with barrels of English ale 'decocted from choice fat grain, as a gift for the French who wondered at such an invention – a drink most wholesome, clear of all dregs, rivalling wine in colour, and surpassing it in savour' (quoted by H. A. Monckton, op. cit.). This drink would not have contained hops, but sweetness or bitterness could have been added by means of honey and such plants as (according to Geoffrey Grigson) bog myrtle, yarrow, ground ivy (hence the plant's former names alehoof and tunhoof) sage and alecost.

Brewing was carried out in the home, the manor-house and in the alehouse. All large establishments had their own breweries. That of Queen's College, Oxford, founded in 1340, continued brewing right up to 1939. Traces of monastic breweries are still to be seen in the ruins of the great abbeys. At Fountains Abbey the malthouse alone was 60 feet square, and the brewery could produce 60 barrels of strong ale every ten days. If my calculations are correct that comes out at 1,728 pints a day. At Canterbury the brewhouse of the Benedictine Priory of Christchurch is as massively imposing as ever, though no longer put to its original use. The usual ration for the monks was at least eight pints a day – much of it probably small (weak) beer.

Domestic brewing was also on a substantial scale. In *A Description of England*, 1577, William Harrison said that his

wife and her maid-servants brewed 200 gallons a month.
This is the equivalent of about 50 pints a day, an impressive
quantity for a fairly modest household.

There were also professional brewers, most of them
women. The word brewster, incidentally, is the female form
of brewer, as baxter is of baker, and spinster of spinner.
Of the 252 tax-paying traders in Faversham in 1327, no
fewer than 84 were ale-wives. Perhaps Faversham was no
more typical then than it is today, when that delightful
small town has the only two breweries left in Kent, a
county that quite recently had as many as was fitting to a
hop-growing area.

With the professional brewer came the need to curb his
(or her) behaviour. In 1267 Henry III had introduced the
Assize of Bread and Ale to maintain the quality of these
vital commodities: prices and quality were controlled, and
to prevent short measures ale had to be sold in pots bearing
the official stamp. This did not stop brewers continuing
in their wicked ways, as we can see from Langland's
complaints about false measures and adulterated beer in
the fourteenth century: in *Piers Plowman* he lists those who
'most harm worketh to the poor people' as being brewsters,
baxters, butchers and cooks, all deserving punishment in the
pillory.

In the fourteenth century an attempt at consumer
protection was made by instituting the post of ale-conner
or ale-taster. The job involved going round making sure
that ale was not being adulterated. H. A. Monckton
describes the ale-conner's method thus:

The official ale-taster wore leather breeches and there
is a story which tells of his test for the quality of the
product. He would draw a tankard of ale, pour it on to
a wooden bench and then sit in the pool he had made.
He would talk and drink for half an hour being extremely
careful not to shift his position. At the end of this time
he would make to rise. If his breeches stuck to the place

whereon he sat, the ale was not considered to be of the highest quality as it revealed that it had a high sugar content. The object of fermentation is to convert sugar into alcohol, and therefore if the ale-taster's breeches did not stick to the bench he could pronounce the ale as good.

This story is repeated by virtually all authors of books about beer, both before and since Mr Monckton, though some tell us that if the leather breeches stuck to the bench the ale was of the *right* quality. Doubtless one version or the other will continue to be narrated in all future books on the subject, but I must record the fact that I have searched in vain for any evidence to support a story which, however colourful, seems highly improbable. Why go to the extra-ordinary trouble of sitting motionless and risking a damp bottom (or worse) when you could achieve the same result with a piece of leather that contained some reasonably heavy object other than an ale-conner? Furthermore, anything with a sugar content high enough to be detected by this peculiar test would be so sweet that only a very eccentric ale-conner would choose to register it with his bottom rather than his taste-buds. This is of course what he did, and on a generous scale too, if the ale-conner in *The Cobbler of Canterbury* was at all typical:

A nose he had that gan show,
What liquor he loved I trow;
For he had before long seven yeare
Been of the towne the ale-conner.

That his services of consumer protection were needed – however he carried them out – is made clear by the climax of one of the fourteenth-century Chester miracle plays, where we find that a special fate is reserved for the brewster. Christ redeems the various characters from damnation, all except one who admits:

Some time I was a taverner
A gentle gossip, and a tapster

Of wine and ale, a trusty brewer
  Which woe hath me bewrought.
Of cans I kept no true measure,
My cups I sold at my pleasure,
Deceiving many a creature,
  Tho' my ale were nought.
Demons carry her off to Hell and the play ends.

The fifteenth and sixteenth centuries saw the most important change in the history of British brewing, namely the introduction of hops and the change from ale to beer. Hop-growing in Central Europe goes back to at least the reign of Charlemagne. There are records of ninth-century hop-growing in the Prince-Bishopric of Freising in the Southern Hallertau district and in Lower Bavaria. Hop-growing rapidly spread throughout Bavaria and other parts of what is now Germany and by the thirteenth century hops were well established throughout northern Europe.

The Romans brought hops to Britain for use as vegetables rather than for brewing. Thereafter there is no mention of them for several centuries. Their return is recorded in the rhyme,

  Hops, Reformation, bays and beer
  Came into England all in one year.

In other versions the first line lists 'Hops and turkeys, carp and beer' and 'Turkeys, carps, hops, pickerel and beer'. All are inaccurate, since hops were both used and grown here well before the Reformation, and pickerel were certainly known in medieval times. The rhyme does at least associate hops and beer, thereby implying a distinction from the un-hopped ale. The meanings of the words *ale* and *beer* overlap considerably, and change at different times in history. So far as possible I shall follow the convention of using *ale* to refer to the ancient unhopped drink, and *beer* for the hopped one.

English soldiers could well have acquired the taste for

hops while fighting in the Low Countries in the fourteenth century, and having done so created a demand for the new drink on their return home. At any rate a hopped malt liquor was imported to Winchelsea in 1400, and shortly afterwards the hops themselves must have been imported. There is mention of brewers of beer (*birra*), as distinct from ale, in Hythe in 1419, but it was probably not until the early sixteenth century that the plant itself became a naturalized growth here, being grown in Kent by Flemish settlers.

The advantages of the hopped drink, both to the brewer and the customer, were so great that beer was bound to supplant ale eventually. The drinker liked the flavour, and for the brewer hops had the useful property of clarifying the wort, giving the beer a good head and helping it to keep better. Reynold Scot in *A Perfite Platforme for a Hoppe Garden*, 1574, noted that

> If your ale may endure a fortnight, your beer through the benefit of the hop shall continue a month, and what grace it yieldeth to the taste, all men may judge that have sense in their mouths. And if controversy be betwixt Beer and Ale, which of them shall have the place of pre-eminence, it sufficeth for the glory and commendation of the Beer that, here in our own country, ale giveth place unto it and that most part of our countrymen do abhor and abandon ale as a loathsome drink . . .

Without the preservative ingredient of hops, ale would probably not have been fully fermented, would therefore contain sugars that had not been turned into alcohol, and so would be extremely sweet. Fortunately nothing like it is brewed today – at least for commercial purposes: on a visit to the Brewing Research Centre at Lyttell Hall, Nutfield, Surrey, I sampled a malt liquor which for experimental reasons had been brewed without hops. It didn't taste at all nice. However, ale was doubtless spiced with other things to make it palatable, and there were, then as now, defenders of real ale.

Though the supremacy of the new drink was inevitable, it was not achieved without a struggle. In 1424 brewers using hops were accused of adulteration, though in 1436 a Royal Writ of Henry VI commended beer as 'notable, healthy and temperate'. In spite of this royal approval the new drink was not universally accepted. As late as 1512 the authorities of Shrewsbury were prohibiting the use of the 'wild, pernicious weed, hops', and the following year the brewers of Coventry were ordered not to use hops. In 1530 Henry VIII ordered his brewer in Eltham not to add hops or brimstone to the ale. Why he should have wanted to add brimstone I'm not sure, but it was no worse than some of the things brewers were using, as we can see from the poem in which John Skelton penned the greatest denunciation of a brewer ever made. Written in about 1517, it is called 'The Tunnyng of Elynour Rummyng' (tunning means putting into tuns, or casks, and therefore by extension brewing). The poem was apparently based on fact, for a real Alianora Romyng is known to have been alive and brewing in Leatherhead in 1525. According to Skelton she was not good-looking:

> Her lothely lere
> Is nothynge clere,
> But ugly of chere,
> Droupy and drowsy,
> Scurvy and lowsy;
> Her face all bowsy,
> Comely crynklyd,
> Lyke a rost pygges eare
> Brysteled with here.
>
> Her nose somdele hoked
> And camously croked,
> Never stoppynge
> But ever droppynge;
> Her skynne lose and slacke,

Greuyned lyke a sacke;
With a croked backe.

In spite of her appearance Elynour's brews were highly
thought of. Skelton tells us she brewed 'noppy ale': noppy
means having a head, foaming, strong, and is a description
of Elynour's ale that is also given to it by a hag called
Sybil, who is as repulsive as Elynour herself:

'This ale,' sayd she, 'is noppy;
Let us syppe and soppy,
And not spyll a droppy,
For so mote I hoppy,
It coleth well my croppy [throat].'

Considering Elynour's brewing methods it is surprising
that the ale was even drinkable, let alone noppy. Hens
ran about her mash-vat and

. . . they go to roust
Streyght over the ale joust,
And donge, when it commes,
In the ale tunnes.
Than Elynour taketh
The mashe bolle and shaketh
The hennes donge away,
And skommeth it into a tray
Whereas the yeest is,
With her maungy fystis.
And somtyme she blennes
The donge of her hennes
And the ale togyder
And sayth, 'Gossyp, come hyder,
This ale shal be thycker
And floure [froth, ferment] the more quycker.'

Hops would seem very innocuous by comparison with
Elynour's ingredients, but they continued to have their
adversaries for many years. Andrew Boorde compares
beer most unfavourably with ale in his *A Dietary of Health*
of about 1542. Ale, he says,

is made of malte and water; and they the which do put any other thynge to ale than is rehersed, except yest, barme or godesgood, doth sofyticat theyr ale. Ale for an Englysche man is a naturall drinke. Ale must have these propertyes: it must be fresshe and cleare, it muste not be ropy or smoky, nor it must have no weft nor tayle. Ale should not be dronke under V days olde.

The upstart beer is correspondingly disparaged as being fit only for foreigners:

Bere is made of malte, of hoppes, and water; it is the naturall drynke for a Dutche man, and now of lete dayes it is much used in England to the detryment of many Englysshe people; specyally it killeth them the which be troubled with the colyke; and the stone and the strangulion; for the drynke is a colde drynke, yet it doth make a man fat, and doth inflate the bely, as it doth appere by the Dutche men's faces and belyes.

Throughout most of the sixteenth century it is ale rather than beer that is mostly praised, as in the song in *Gammer Gurton's Needle*, 1575:

Back and side go bare, go bare,
    Both foot and hand go cold:
But, belly, God send thee good ale enough,
    Whether it be new or old.

I cannot eat but little meat,
    My stomach is not good;
But sure I think that I can drink
    With him that wears a hood.
Though I go bare, take ye no care,
    I am nothing a-cold;
I stuff my skin so full within
    Of jolly good ale and old.

Shakespeare usually refers to ale in terms of praise – 'A quart of ale is a dish for a king' (*The Winter's Tale*) – and disparagingly of that 'poor creature, small beer'. Robert

Greene in his *Quip for an Upstart Courtier*, 1592, is still more scathing, though perhaps more at the expense of brewers than beer:

> And you, masser Brewer, that growe to be worth forty thousand pounds by your selling of soden water, what subtilty have you in making your beer, to spare the malt, and put in the more of the hop to make your drink, (be barley never so cheap) not a whit the stronger, yet never sell a whit the more measure for money, you can when you have taken all the heart of the malt away, then clap on store of water 'tis cheap enough, and mash a tunning of small beer, that it scours a man's maw like rennish wine: in your conscience how many barrels draw you out of a quarter of malt? fie, fie, I conceal your falsehood, lest I should be too broad in setting down your faults.

Nevertheless, by the second half of the sixteenth century it was evident that hops were here to stay. Edward VI, far from discouraging their use as his unpleasant father had done, gave hop-growers special privileges. First in the hop-growing south-east, and then over the rest of the country, beer gradually replaced ale. Paul Hentzner in *A Journey to England*, 1598, says that 'the general drink is beer, which is prepared from barley, and is excellently well tasted, but strong and what soon fuddles.' The best medical opinion was that in addition to its pleasant taste beer had all kinds of beneficial effects, such as cleansing the body and purging the blood. John Gerard's *Herbal*, 1597, declares that 'The manifold vertues in Hops do manifestly argue the holsome-ness of Beere above Ale; for the Hops rather make it a Phisicall drinke to keepe the body in health, than an ordi-narie drinke for the quenching of our thirst.'

With Henry VIII's dissolution of the monasteries the monastic breweries, which had been the biggest in the country, mostly went too. Some managed to continue operations independently: Joule's brewery in Stone, for example, founded by monks in the twelfth century, survived right up to 1974 when it was killed off by Henry VIII's spiritual descendant, Bass Charrington.

Until the seventeenth century home-brewing still dominated in country areas but was going out of fashion in towns, where beer was increasingly made by innkeepers. The professional brewer made his appearance too, and on a big scale. Greene had spoken of brewers worth £40,000, and in the seventeenth century professional brewers became men of considerable substance and social standing. John Bide, for example, was Sheriff of London in 1647. He was a brewer of quality, if Samuel Pepys's connoisseurship is anything to go by. Pepys repeatedly sought out Bide's ale. He notes in his diary for 17 August 1667: 'Thence home and went as far as Mile End with Sir W. Pen, whose coach took him up there for his country-house; and after having drunk there, at the Rose and Crowne, a good house for Alderman Bide's ale, we parted . . .' A few days later, 24 August, was the day of 'the peace between us and the States of the United Provinces, and also of the King of France and Denmarke', an event which Pepys celebrated by going with his wife to Mile End, 'and there drank Bide's ale, and so home.' On 30 September he is again 'drinking (as usual) at Mile End of Byde's ale'.

Bide was not the only brewer to achieve wealth and position. Several became Members of Parliament, and those knighted included Felix Feast, John Parsons, John Lade, John Friend, Charles Cox and George Meggott. John Taylor, the self-styled 'Water-Poet' (1580–1653) testifies in characteristically feeble verse to the growing prosperity of the brewers:

> Thus Water boils, parboils, and mundifies,
> Clears, cleanses, clarifies and purifies.
> But as it purgeth us from filth and stink,
> We must remember that it makes us drink,

Metheglin, Bragget, Beer and headstrong Ale,
(That can put colour in a visage pale)
By which means many Brewers are grown rich,
And in estates may soar a lofty pitch.
Men of good rank and place, and much command,
Who have (by sodden Water) purchased land.

Taylor was a last-ditch defender of ale. In his memorably titled *Ale Ale-vated into the Ale-titude* (1651) he condemns beer as 'a Dutch boorish liquor . . . a saucy intruder in this Land,' whereas ale 'makes the footman's head and heels so light that he seems to fly as he runs; it is the warmest lining of a naked man's coat; it satiates and assuageth hunger and cold'. He adds that it is a specific against melancholy, *Tremor cordis*, maladies of the spleen, gripings of the guts, and stone in the bladder or kidneys; it relieves the agonies of gout, sciatica, fevers, agues and rheums, and provokes urine wonderfully.

By the end of the century the distinction between ale and beer was becoming blurred. From James Lightbody's *Every Man his Own Gauger*, 1695, it appears that ale too was hopped at this period, though more lightly than beer. In his instructions for brewing he says that 'The quantity of hops you are to use for Ale is 3 Pound to 8 Bushels of Malt; if it be Beer, you put 6 pound to 8 bush.' Lightbody's book is of some importance in the history of brewing because of its mention of isinglass as a fining agent: 'Take the whites of 10 eggs and mix with wheat Flower and add thereto, a spoonful of the Jelly of Isinglass, and a small quantity of Niter, and it will preserve, clear and feed the Beer to Admiration.' Histories of brewing all give credit for the earliest mention of isinglass in brewing to Michael Combrune in the middle of the eighteenth century. Lightbody's book is proof that it was in use at least half a century before that.

The seventeenth century was an age of song; the eighteenth

was one of drink. People of all ages and social classes, men and women alike, were drunk most of the time. Those who could afford it inebriated themselves with port and claret; for the poor the means was gin.

Apothecaries in Salerno had discovered the art of distilling some time around the year 1100, but its application spread only very slowly, and rarely for use in the making of drinks. Hieronymus Braunschweig's *The Vertuose Boke of Distyllacion* was published in an English translation in 1527, and it is known that spirits were consumed as prophylactics in the plague year of 1593.

In 1689 William of Orange was accompanied to England by a Dutch distilled drink which was flavoured with juniper – Dutch *genever*, hence *gin*. Acts of Parliament of 1690 and 1703 deprived the Disillers' Company of its monopoly and made it legal for anyone to distil spirits from English corn and sell them without even a licence. The idea was to reduce the import of brandy as part of the economic war against France. In the event it was not the French but the English who suffered. Whereas the sale of beer had been restricted for centuries, that of the new drink was not, and since the duty was only twopence a gallon, and was often evaded anyway, gin was absurdly cheap. Production of spirits went up from half a million gallons a year in 1684 to 2 million in 1700, over 5 million in 1735 and around 20 million at the height of the epidemic in 1740–42. This was the time of 'Drunk for a penny, dead drunk for twopence, clean straw for nothing.' In London there were twice as many burials as baptisms, and in some parts of the city as many as one house in four was a gin-shop. The squalor was unspeakable, and it is no exaggeration to say that spirits-drinking in the middle of the eighteenth century very nearly destroyed the entire structure of society. In *An Enquiry into the Cause of the late Increase of Robbers*, 1751, Fielding refers to the drunkenness caused by:

that poison called *gin*: which I have great reason to

think, is the principal sustenance (if it may be so called)
of more than a hundred thousand people of this metropolis. Many of these wretches there are who swallow pints
of this poison within the twenty-four hours: the dreadful
effects of which I have the misfortune every day to see,
and to smell too.

To call it poison was perfectly accurate. The late Sir Jack
Drummond in his fascinating book *The Englishman's Food*
quotes a recipe for the kind of thing sold by the less reputable
gin-shops; it includes oil of vitriol (sulphuric acid), oil of
almonds, oil of turpentine, spirits of wine, lump sugar,
lime water, rose water, alum and salt of tartar.

A pamphlet of 1736 describes a place near East Smith-
field which had a large empty room at the back into which
the customers, as they became intoxicated, were 'laid
together in heaps promiscuously, men, women, and children,
till they recover their senses, when they proceed to drink
on, or, having spent all they had, go out to find wherewithal
to return to the same drunken pursuit; and how they acquire
more money the sessions paper too often acquaints us.'

The best-known, and most vivid, account of the squalor
of the gin epidemic is Hogarth's 'Gin Lane'. In this scene
of degraded urban filth there are people gnawing at bones,
dying of hunger. We see through a window into a house
where a man has hanged himself. Another corpse is being
lifted into a coffin in the street. The central figure is a half-
naked woman with terrible sores on her legs, smiling
drunkenly as her baby falls unheeded over a parapet.
Even the houses seem to be inebriated, as they totter, reel
and collapse in disrepair. The only houses in good condition
are those of the pawnbroker and the undertaker. A rhyme
beneath the engraving denounces the cause:

> Gin! curs'd fiend with fury fraught,
>   Makes human race a prey,
> It enters by a deadly draught,
>   And steals our life away.

Hogarth's 'Beer Street', by contrast, is a picture of health and welfare in which cheerful and prosperous people go soberly and industriously about their business. The buildings are as well-preserved as the people – all except the pawnbroker's: his house is tumbling down and the three-balled sign has almost fallen off. The rhyme beneath the engraving extols the benign drink that has brought about this pleasant state of affairs:

> Beer! happy produce of our isle,
>   Can sinewy strength impart,
> And wearied with fatigue and toil,
>   Can cheer each manly heart.
>
> Labour and art upheld by thee,
>   Successfully advance,
> We quaff thy balmy juice with glee,
>   And water leave to France.
>
> Genius of health! thy grateful taste
>   Rivals the cup of Jove,
> And warms each English generous breast
>   With liberty and love.

Unfortunately 'Beer Street' was largely wishful thinking, a Utopian dream of what might be achieved if sobriety broke out. The houses of 'Gin Lane' were closer to mid-eighteenth-century reality.

In 1736 the Government attempted to improve things by introducing a Gin Act which slightly raised the tax. All this achieved was widespread rioting. The £50 licence for retailers was prohibitively expensive and so easily evaded that there is only evidence of two of these licences being issued: the citizens concerned must have been of positively eccentric law-abidingness. It was not until 1751 that a real effort was made to control the evil. This time the tax was raised considerably and the sale of gin restricted. There followed a reduction in the consumption of spirits, but this was probably due less to legislation than to a steep rise in the price of grain and other fermentable materials which almost trebled the price of gin.

By 1758 one H. Jackson was writing in *An Essay on Bread* that 'Beer, commonly call'd Porter, is almost become the universal Cordial of the Populace . . .' This 'Universal Cordial' was first brewed by Ralph Harwood at Shoreditch in 1722. A popular drink at the time was a mixture called 'three-threads'. There is some disagreement as to the precise constituents: whether it was one-third pale ale, one-third brown and one-third old; or pale, new brown and stale brown; or pale, brown and small; or pale, strong and twopenny. At any rate 'three-threads' involved taking beer from three separate casks. This was obviously a troublesome business for the publican. Harwood's new drink was, so to speak, ready mixed, a single beer combining the qualities of the three. From this it took the name 'entire butt' or 'entire'. It quickly won popularity with London porters, and thus acquired the name by which it was to become generally known – porter.

It is impossible to say precisely what eighteenth-century porter tasted like. Bottled Guinness is probably the nearest thing to porter that is brewed today. From the beginning it was evidently bitter and strong, made from slightly scorched malt, which gave it blackness and thickness. London water was especially suited for its manufacture, and for the brewer it had the advantage that it could be produced in extremely large quantities and in hotter weather than other beer. Whereas the light beer of Burton was only brewed from October to May, the London porter-brewers carried right on from the beginning of September to the middle of June. For these and other technical reasons the invention of porter was conducive to the creation of very large breweries. Peter Mathias writes in his definitive study of the subject that porter was the first beer technically suited for mass production and was an invention equivalent in its industry to coke-smelted iron, mule-spun muslin in textiles or 'pressed-ware' pottery.

Porter needed long maturing. The consequent risk of air-borne infection was reduced by storing it in extremely large vats, the size of which meant that they had a smaller exposed surface in proportion to quantity than a small container would have. This was sensible enough, but the porter-brewers allowed the building of huge vats to get out of hand. They vied with one another to build the biggest, rather as the rival families of San Gimignano tried to outdo one another by building more and higher towers. When one of Thrale's new vats was completed the event was celebrated by a hundred people dining in it. In about 1790 Meux built one that was 60 feet wide and 23 feet high: 200 people dined in this one, while another 200 drank to its success. In 1795 he built one twice as big, holding 20,000 barrels. The rivalry continued into the nineteenth century and, as is the way of such things, ended in tears. On 17 October 1814 an enormous vat burst at Henry Meux's Horse Shoe Brewery near Tottenham Court Road. One can get some concept of the size of the thing from the fact that the deluge swept away the walls of the brewery, demolished nearby buildings and killed eight people by 'drowning, injury, poisoning by the porter fumes or drunkenness.'

Thanks to porter and the abatement of the gin epidemic the brewers became immensely wealthy. *The Gentleman's Magazine* refers in 1763 to 'Brewers pining at the hardships they labour under and rolling away in their coaches and six to their several villas to drown their grief in burgundy and champagne.' There was real money in beer and it took a rare kind of incompetence to make a mess of things – the kind of incompetence possessed by Henry Thrale. When his brewery was being sold up after his death, Dr Johnson (who was involved in the transaction through his close association with Mrs Thrale) remarked, 'Sir, we are not here to sell a parcel of boilers and vats, but the potentiality of growing rich beyond the dreams of avarice.' The brewery went for £135,000.

The great breweries were founded in the eighteenth century. In London Thrale started in 1729, Whitbread in 1742, Charrington in 1766 and Courage in 1789; in Burton Worthington started brewing in 1744 and William Bass in 1777; George's was founded in Bristol in 1788; Ind's at Romford in 1779; and in Ireland Smithwick's was founded in 1710 and Arthur Guinness in 1759.

The major London breweries in the eighteenth century were big even by modern standards, and getting bigger all the time. In 1760 five London breweries were each producing more than 50,000 barrels a year: in 1781 six were brewing more than 80,000. The great brewing fortunes were based on producing a high quality commodity at a competitive price. To secure their profit margins the brewers had to be able to ensure uniform quality. This was made possible by considerable improvements in the understanding and technology of brewing. As brewers became more scientific they began to make specialized use of their available materials. The water of Burton-on-Trent contains calcium sulphate (gypsum) and this was found to be particularly suitable for brewing pale ale; London water, which has a high proportion of calcium carbonate and some sodium chloride, was better suited to stout and porter. By the end of the century brewers had learned how to add or take away these salts to suit the beer they were brewing. This meant that stout could be produced in Burton and light ales in London.

By the early nineteenth century temperature control had made it possible to brew throughout the year instead of only from autumn to spring. Books such as Michael Combrune's *Essay on Brewing* (1758) and *Theory and Practice of Brewing* (1762), and John Richardson's *Philosophical Principles of the Science of Brewing* (1784) made the first attempts at giving systematic accounts of the principles of brewing. Whereas in the past temperatures were taken by such rule-of-thumb approximations as 'blood heat' or 'the temperature that can just be tolerated by the elbow', now the thermometer was used, and further precise measurements could be made with the saccharometer (hydrometer). Gradually the way in which yeast operates became understood. In 1680 Leeuwenhoek sent the Royal Society descriptions and drawings of yeast cells he saw through his microscope. Lavoisier (1743–94) put forward the theory of fermentation, showing that as sugar disappeared, alcohol, carbon dioxide and acetic acid were formed. Gay-Lussac (1770–1850) produced an equation that a molecule of sugar can be broken down to two molecules of alcohol and two molecules of CO_2. It was not until 1857 that Pasteur was to discover the full functioning of yeast, and to add the microscope to the thermometer and hydrometer among the brewer's standard equipment.

While improved knowledge and technology meant that the big brewers were increasingly able to produce beer of uniform quality, the smaller ones, especially in the country, continued to use hit-and-miss methods: their beer varied enormously in quality, and there were widespread complaints about village brewers.

Beer retained into the nineteenth century the virtuous image it had earned as the alternative not only to the demon gin but also to the extremely expensive imported drinks, coffee and tea. These both arrived in the middle of the seventeenth century – Pepys records in 1660 drinking 'a cup of tea (a China drink) of which I had never drank before'. In spite of its extremely high price, it rapidly became fashionable among all classes, though it also had its opponents. Jonas Hanway, the first Englishman to carry an umbrella, attacked tea in 1757 as 'an epidemical disease . . . You may see labourers who are mending the road drinking their tea . . . it is even . . . sold out of cups to haymakers . . . were they the sons of tea-sippers who won the fields of

Crécy and Agincourt or dyed the Danube's shores with Gallic blood?'

William Cobbett followed Hanway in being strongly pro-beer and anti-tea, and in 1822 Brougham denounced tea for not contributing to the cultivation of a single acre of English land. Beer, on the other hand, was a 'moral species of beverage,' full of patriotic, un-French, un-Papist, un-foreign associations, as much part of our island heritage as Magna Carta. 'What two ideas,' asked Sydney Smith, 'are more inseparable than beer and Britannia?'

Unfortunately there were doubts about how wholesome some of the beer was. Like many others of this and other periods, Cobbett complained about the adulteration of beer. In spite of various Acts of Parliament the brewers continued to water, adulterate and even drug the beer. The anonymous author of *The London and Country Brewer* (1738) had described the practices of unscrupulous brewers who used a poisonous drug called *cocculus indicus* to give bitterness and a heady character to weak beer. He describes it as being 'of the nature of deadly nightshade'.

An anonymous pamphlet of 1757 called *Poison Detected: Frightful Truths: and Alarming to the British Metropolis* speaks of the use of acids and other unpleasant substances in brewing. Accum's notable book on food adulteration in 1820 was still accusing the brewers of using *cocculus indicus* and other harmful substances such as sulphuric acid for the 'maturing' of porter.

Coinciding with these complaints about adulterated beer came a recurrence of the gin epidemic, which had considerably abated during the Napoleonic wars. Mathias shows that whereas consumption of spirits increased between 1722 and 1833 from 0·5 gallons per head to 0·9, and that of tea from 1 oz per head to 2·3 lb, beer declined from 1 barrel per head to 0·5. The Beer Act of 1830 was intended to get people to drink manly, patriotic, English beer instead of pernicious spirits and tea, and also to weaken the grip that the brewers were already tightening on the retail trade through the tied house system. Its proponents hoped that it would break the power of the licensing magistrates, some of whom were in the pockets of the big brewers. Sydney Smith told Brougham in 1828 that the system was 'one of the most enormous and scandalous Tyrannies ever exercised upon any people', and wrote elsewhere that 'We *must* have a small massacre of magistrates: nothing else will do.'

What the Beer Act did was to allow anyone to sell beer merely by paying a two-guinea excise duty, and at the same time to abolish the duty on beer. It was a free trade act intended to keep down prices and curb drunkenness and smuggling. The immediate, and most conspicuous, result was that instead of everyone getting drunk on gin everyone got drunk on beer. A few days after the Bill was passed, Sydney Smith wrote in a letter: 'The new Beer Bill has begun its operations. Everybody is drunk. Those who are not singing are sprawling. The sovereign people are in a beastly state.'

In fairness to the free traders, they had predicted that the new law would be followed by a temporary increase in drunkenness, and over the next hundred years drinking and drunkenness certainly declined. How much credit should go to the Beer Act and how much to such factors as the temperance movement, hygienic water supplies and higher living standards is doubtful.

At the beginning of the nineteenth century there was a considerable variety of kinds of beer: porter, brown stout, Reading beer, Amber beer or twopenny, winter beer, London ale, Windsor ale, Welch ale, Scotch ale, Wirtenburg ale, Hock, scurvy-glass ale, table beer and shipping beer are some of those mentioned. In the course of the century the distribution of the main kinds of beer began to change, with the light Burton beers beginning to supplant London's porter. Between 1831 and 1847 the production of Bass in Burton increased by six times. Porter, on the other hand, which had accounted for three-quarters of London's beer in 1863, was down to only a quarter by the end of the century. In self-defence the London brewers had to produce the lighter beer (or ale, as it was being called again). Whitbread, for one, started doing so in 1834.

In spite of these changes in demand and supply the brewing industry continued to flourish like the green bay tree, as Mrs Micawber so movingly testifies in *David Copperfield* (1849–50):

'I will not conceal from you, my dear Mr Copperfield,' said Mrs Micawber, 'that *I* have long felt the Brewing business to be particularly adapted to Mr Micawber. Look at Barclay, Perkins! Look at Truman, Hanbury and Buxton! It is on that extensive footing that Mr Micawber, I know from my knowledge of him, is calculated to shine; and the profits, I am told, are e-NOR-mous! But if Mr Micawber cannot get into those firms – which decline to answer his letters, when he offers his services even in an inferior capacity – what is the use of dwelling upon the idea? None.'

Poor Mrs Micawber! Poor Mr Micawber! Had a more sympathetic response greeted his letters of application, who knows but that his name might have ranked with those great nineteenth-century brewers celebrated by C. S. Calverley:

O Beer! O Hodgson, Guinness, Allsopp, Bass!
    Names that should be on every infant's tongue!
Shall days and months and years and centuries pass,
    And still your merits be unrecked, unsung?
Oh! I have gazed into my foaming glass,
    And wished that lyre could yet again be strung
Which once rang prophet-like through Greece, and
                                          taught her
Misguided sons that the best drunk is water.

The above brief history of ale and beer from Hammurabi

to Wilkins Micawber has as far as possible avoided tech-nicalities. This is not so easy when dealing with the twentieth century, since some of the most important developments have had technical causes. Therefore, as both interlude and preparation, the next chapter will look at the way in which beer is brewed and dispensed, the varieties of beer, its ingredients, and so on.

III What's Brewing

1 The national drink

Adults in the United Kingdom drink an average of more than 30 gallons of beer every year, as against less than two gallons of wine. Were one to measure the amount written about the respective drinks in newspapers and books, I imagine that the proportion would be just about reversed. There are good reasons for this. Precisely because we are not a wine-producing country, at least on any significant scale, and are still only becoming a wine-consuming one, fermented grape juice is something foreign and exotic to us, and we readily accept the need for expert guidance to its mysteries. With beer the situation is different. Everyone who goes to a pub once or twice a week and downs a pint or three considers himself to be an authority not only on the declining moral fibre of the nation but also on beer.

Nevertheless, considering the importance of beer to our diet, our social lives and indeed to the economy, it is surprising that writers have not paid more attention to our national drink, for that is what beer has long been. Tea is a relative newcomer, and in many parts of the country water only became safe to drink fairly recently. It could be rendered harmless by the sterilizing effects of fermentation, which is why for centuries weak 'small' beer was the standard drink for all classes and ages at all meals. Since it was weak it could be (and was) consumed in large quantities: at Syon convent in 1371 the nuns were given seven gallons of ale a week each – eight pints a day.

In our more affluent and hygienic times beer retains its importance in our diet, our social lives and national economy.

In 1973 the British people spent some £1,800 million on beer – as against £650 million on milk and dairy foods, and £450 million on bread. About a third of the price of beer is accounted for by tax, and in 1974–5 the Chancellor of the Exchequer took more than £600 million in tax on beer, a rate of more than £18 a second. (In the past the drinker shouldered an even bigger share of the national finances. In 1966-67 tax on alcoholic drinks accounted for 6·7 per cent of total State revenue. In 1839 it was 33 per cent. At the end of the eighteenth century nearly half the revenue came from tax on alcoholic drinks.)

Though in terms of time television accounts for the biggest share of the leisure business, in terms of money this distinction goes to pubs. Some ten per cent of all spending on eating out is accounted for by meals and snacks in pubs, which thereby also represent a significant section of the catering industry.

In 1974 Britain produced 11,094 million pints of beer (38,520,054 barrels). We are the third biggest producer of beer in the world, the 1973 figures being (in million bulk barrels) USA 106·61, West Germany 56·5, UK 37. The 1973 figures for per capita consumption in pints for various countries are

West Germany	258·2
Czechoslovakia	257·6
Belgium	250·8
Luxembourg	231·1
Australia	228·8
Republic of Ireland	221·6
Denmark	220·8
East Germany	198·4
UK	197·1

(source, Brewers' Society)

At the other end of the scale comes Italy with only 24·1 pints per head a year.

The Shorter Oxford Dictionary defines beer as 'an

alcoholic liquor obtained by the fermentation of malt (or other saccharine substance), flavoured with hops or other bitters. Formerly distinguished from *ale* by being hopped; but now generic, including ale and porter.' The definition indicates an important event in the history of the drink that took place with the introduction of hops, but it does not suggest the great diversity of beer. There is at least as much variety among the drinks called beer as among those called wine, the difference between Guinness and lager, for example, being every bit as great as that between hock and claret. In this country we have a greater variety of beer than anywhere else in the world, with our bitters, milds, old ales, winter warmers, stouts, brown and light ales, barley wines and strong ales. There is less variety than there used to be, partly because there are fewer brewers, but there are still reckoned to be 1,500 different beers currently available.

This variety is one distinguishing factor of British beer: the other is that we drink kinds of beer that are virtually unknown in the rest of the world. Outside the British Isles beer means, with only a few exceptions, lager. In Britain the traditional beers in recent centuries have been stout, bitter and mild.

2 The ingredients

YEAST

The essential difference between traditional British beer and lager is in the kind of yeast used. British beer is top-fermented, lager is bottom-fermented. This means that the yeast operates at the top and bottom respectively, British beer being fermented by a yeast called *Saccharomyces cerevisiae*, lager by *Saccharomyces carlsbergensis* (named after the Carlsberg Brewery in Denmark where it was isolated by E. C. Hansen in the nineteenth century). There are still a few top-fermented beers to be found in Holland, Belgium (especially those brewed by Trappist monks), Germany (notably Düsseldorf Alt beer, and Cologne's Kölsch) and Australia, where an excellent top-fermented beer is brewed by Cooper and Sons' Upper Kensington Brewery, Adelaide.

Yeast, a living micro-organism, is the fermenting agent which converts sugar into equal quantities of carbon dioxide and alcohol. During this process it reproduces so prolifically that at the end of fermentation the brewer is left with five to ten times as much yeast as he started with. What is not needed for the next brew is sold off, mostly to manufacturers of yeast extracts, notably Marmite.

The operation of yeast was long a mystery, as is suggested by one of its ancient names, *goddisgoode*. Only in 1680 did Leeuwenhoek, with the aid of a microscope, manage to draw and describe the cells of yeast, but their exact role in fermentation was still not understood. Further discoveries about yeast and fermentation were made by Lavoisier and Gay-Lussac, but it was not till the middle of the nineteenth century that Pasteur finally established that the process of turning sugar into carbon dioxide and alcohol only took place in the presence of living cells of yeast.

MALT

Malt is not, as many people mistakenly suppose, the thick brown substance sold by chemists under such trade names as Virol and Radio Malt. These are extracts of malt. True malt, as used by the brewer, looks almost indistinguishable from barley. A barleycorn is rather like an egg: it has a hard exterior which contains an embryo and the food on which the seed will live until it has established itself in the soil and found independent sources of nourishment. When a corn is planted in the soil, the dampness and warmth cause it to germinate, and enzymes change the insoluble starch in the corn into soluble starch. The maltster reproduces this process in a speeded-up version. He steeps the barley in water, then heaps it on the floor. As soon as germination begins, he spreads the barley out on the malting floor. When he judges the process to have gone far enough he stops it by lightly cooking it in a kiln. When the rootlets have been removed the malt (as it now is) looks just like the barley-corn it started out as: however, if you put a grain between your teeth you will find that whereas the barleycorn is stone-hard, the malt is crunchy and tastes like Horlicks. The soluble starch in the malt is later converted into sugar by the mashing process, and the sugar is in turn changed by fermentation into carbon dioxide and alcohol.

HOPS

Two families of the hemp genus (*cannabaceae*) are now naturalized in Britain. The more recent arrival is *cannabis sativa*, which is sometimes found growing wild on waste ground, and is also illegally sown as a source of marijuana. Equally controversial in its time was the related *humulus lupulus*. The hop is a tall climbing perennial, square-stemmed, with hairs that are rough enough to leave a picker's hands raw with scratches. In this country it grows wild in hedgerows and is cultivated in hop-fields where it twines clockwise up strings to a length of as much as twenty feet. These strings are made of coir yarn, of which a hop garden of 1,000 acres will need about 15,000 miles each year.

The Romans brought hops here to eat as vegetables, snipping off the young shoots in summer and preparing them in the manner of asparagus. I gather this is still done in Czechoslovakia and that, though laborious to prepare, *Hopfensalat* is excellent to eat. When the Romans left the hops seem to have gone with them, and as we saw in the previous chapter, they had to be reintroduced in the fifteenth century for use in brewing.

Although the arrival of hops in Britain was not at first welcomed their advantages were too many for them to be resisted indefinitely. For the brewer, hops are useful because they help to clarify and preserve the beer; for the consumer, their attraction is their bitterness, flavour and aroma. Flemish immigrants established hop-growing in Kent in the first half of the sixteenth century and we are now one of the major hop-producing countries. About a third of the hops are grown in Herefordshire and Worcestershire, the rest in Hampshire, Sussex and Kent.

'Kent, sir,' said Mr Jingle, 'everybody knows Kent – apples, cherries, hops and women.' Having been brought up in Kent I am probably prejudiced in thinking it the most beautiful county in England, but that it is beautiful will not be denied, and hops have contributed to that beauty. For one thing they have given us the oast houses in which the hops are dried. There are few lovelier sights than coming round a corner of the road at Beltring and suddenly seeing the magnificent collection of oasts at Whitbread's hop farm. Siegfried Sassoon described them in *Memoirs of a Fox-hunting Man*:

> It was unusual to find more than two hop kilns on a farm, but there was one which had twenty and its company of white cowls was clearly visible from our house on the hill; I would count them over and over again and Dixon would agree it was a wonderful sight. I felt that almost anything might happen in a world which could show me twenty hop kilns neatly arranged in a field.

He should have counted once more, because there are twenty-five kilns and cowls, not twenty. A group of four houses, each with five oasts, carries twenty tiled cones, each crowned by a gleaming white cowl, all pointing in the same direction like some kind of ancient early-warning system; standing slightly apart, another great building with an immense tiled roof bears another five white cowls. Apart from this quibble, one can wholeheartedly agree with Sassoon that it is indeed a wonderful sight. Though the Beltring oast houses are probably the most spectacular, others are to be found all over the county making their distinctive contribution to the Kent landscape. Many have now been converted for domestic purposes.

Another major contribution to the beauty of Kent is the hop-fields themselves, where the plants grow in ranks and files of parade-ground precision. Orwell describes them well in his novel *A Clergyman's Daughter*: 'The hop-bines, tall climbing plants like runner beans enormously magnified, grew in green leafy lanes, with the hops dangling from them in pale green bunches like gigantic grapes. When the wind stirred them they shook forth a fresh, bitter scent of sulphur and cool beer.' At that time hop-picking was all done by hand, mostly by families from the East End of London who would come down to the same farm year after year, some 40,000 of them in all. It was exhausting work, but for the working people of London it was also a holiday. For many it was the only way a family could afford to go away together, and the only experience of the countryside they ever had. You still find Londoners who will reminisce happily about their hop-picking experiences, and will compare them favourably with the package tours to Torremolinos that have replaced them. Two recent autobiographies by Londoners contain fond memories of pre-war hop-picking: Louis Heren's *Growing Up Poor in London* and Johnny Speight's *It Stands to Reason*.

Nowadays the hand-pickers have been replaced by machines. With better wages elsewhere and cheap holiday travel, the average age of the hand-pickers went up steadily every year, until it looked as though there would soon be only a few grannies left. At the same time the machines became more economic and increasingly efficient. Today virtually all hops are picked by machine, and the casual labour is provided mostly by students accumulating money for the beginning of the academic year.

There have been other changes too. You don't often see men on stilts in the hop-fields now: stilts have been replaced by a crow's-nest on the back of a tractor. Many of the famous old hop varieties are on their way out too. The Goldings and the Fuggles (named respectively after a Mr Golding and a Mr Fuggle) are being replaced by new varieties with greater resistance to wilt (rivalled only by gales as the great enemy of the hop-farmer) and high in a substance called alpha-acid which is much prized by the brewer.

Another important change is coming about as a result of EEC regulations. The hop, like the banana and holly and many other plants, is dioecious. That is to say, the unisexual male and female flowers are on separate plants; to put it simply, there are male hops and female hops. The female produces the green flowers that are used by the brewer. If female plants are grown in isolation these flowers are not fertile and hold no seeds, just as hens which don't have a cock living with them lay unfertilized eggs.

On the Continent hop-fields have long consisted only of female plants, and in order to preserve their virginity the male has been ruthlessly hunted down. It is an offence to have a male hop growing on your land, there are mug shots of the male hop in police stations, and in Belgium he has been outlawed by royal proclamation. In England, by contrast, far from being treated like a felon, the male hop has for more than 500 years led a pampered and polygamous life in the fields, each male being surrounded by some 200 females. In his presence the hop-flowers are fertilized and seeded. The seed, which may amount to 15 to 20 per cent of the yield, is of no use to the brewer, and in lager-brewing may be positively a nuisance. On the other hand, some claim that seeded hops have some extra protection from the diseases to which hops are exposed in our climate. Whatever the pros and cons, the Ministry of

Agriculture seems set on seedlessness, and the male is to be eradicated. This will be a tricky job, since so many are growing wild in the hedgerows. They will never surrender. As far as the beer drinker is concerned, we are assured that the change to seedless hops will make no difference to the beer. We shall see.

Hops help beer to keep, and they also give it bitterness and flavour. If you walk within half a mile of a brewery you cannot fail to notice the smell of hops. Unfortunately they are not always so noticeable in the beer itself. The aroma of hops is one of the most delightful known to the human nose, but hops are expensive things and while the amount of beer brewed has gone up in recent years, the volume of hops used has not increased in proportion. The brewers explain this by saying that the new varieties of hops have a higher bittering factor than the old ones, and also that they have improved their usage of hops. This may be so, but it seems to me that beer tastes less hoppy than it used to, an impression confirmed by older consumers. This is especially true of the beer produced by the Big Six brewing companies. For outstandingly hoppy beer I would recommend the draught bitters of Brakspear's of Henley-on-Thames, or those of Shepherd Neame of Faversham or King and Barnes of Horsham.

WATER

Brewers always call water 'liquor'. In order to ensure a constant supply of uncontaminated water breweries in the past usually had their own wells, though nowadays most use public water supplies. Local variations in the character of water affect the flavour of beer considerably. It was long ago discovered, for example, that Burton-on-Trent was particularly suited to the production of pale ales on account of the gypsum in the water, while London water, which contains relatively high amounts of calcium carbonate and sodium chloride, was best suited to the brewing of porter and stout. Nowadays the brewer can adjust the water to suit whatever kind of beer he wants to produce by adding or taking away the relevant salts.

OTHER INGREDIENTS

According to the old rhyme

He that buys land buys many stones
He that buys flesh buys many bones
He that buys eggs buys many shells
But he that buys good beer buys nothing else.

In Germany this remains true. In 1516 Count William IV of Bavaria issued a Reinheitsgebot (Purity Law) which allowed the use only of barley, hops and water in the making of beer: this law is still in force throughout the whole of Germany. These were also the only permitted ingredients of brewing in Britain until an Act of 1847 permitted the use of sugar, but as we have already seen unscrupulous brewers had been using far worse things long before that. In the eighteenth century and early nineteenth popular additions were a poisonous drug called *cocculus indicus* (Indian berry) and what H. Jackson described in 1758 as 'green vitriol commonly called copperas or salt of Iron'. It was said that a mixture of alum and copperas would produce a 'head like a Collyflower' – presumably in the beer rather than the consumer. William Cobbett frequently denounced 'beer-doctors' and 'beer-druggists', and in *Cottage Economy* (1821) quotes a recipe for porter from a book on brewing: 'Take one quarter of high-coloured malt, eight pounds of hops, nine pounds of treacle, eight pounds of colour, eight pounds of sliced liquorice-root, two drams of salt of tartar, two ounces of Spanish-liquorice, and half an ounce of capsicum.' That the complaint of adulteration was common at that period is shown by a ballad of about 1825 called 'London Adulterations, or Rogues in Grain, Tea, Coffee, Milk, Beer, Snuff, Mutton, Pork, Gin, Butter, etc.'

> The brewer's a chemist, and that is quite clear,
> We soon find no hops have hopped into his beer;
> 'Stead of malt he from drugs brews his porter and swipes:
> No wonder so oft that we all get the gripes.

(quoted from *A Touch of the Times*, edited by Roy Palmer, Penguin Education).

Complaints about the adulteration of beer by what Dickens called the 'brewhouse-chemist' continued throughout the century. Hardy in *Tess of the d'Urbervilles* (1891) refers to the 'curious compounds sold . . . as beer by the monopolizers of the once independent inns'. As late as the 1930s we find J. B. Morton (Beachcomber) defining beer in his 'Dictionary for Today' as 'A drink made of various chemicals in various proportions'; brewer is 'An almost obsolete word. It now means chemist', and hops are 'An old-fashioned ingredient of beer, before the custom of using chemicals came in'. These later criticisms are largely unjustified, and probably derive from the propaganda of the temperance movement.

Quite recently cobalt sulphate was used in brewing in the United States: this gave a very good head to the beer but a very bad heart to the consumer and after more than 40 people had died its use was banned. In this country, however, most of the additions to beer are not actually injurious to health but are economies which affect flavour. Mr John Young, chairman of Young's of Wandsworth, said in his annual company report for 1974 that 'our definition of beer is that it is brewed from malted barley and hops, and we have no use for wheat flour, rice or potato starch'. These substitutes for malt are politely called 'adjuncts'. At the time of writing the Consumers' Association and the Campaign for Real Ale have both proposed to the Food Standards Committee on Beer that there should be a limit of 30 per cent on adjuncts, or to put it another way, that the 'malt fraction' should be at least 70 per cent. One might have thought that no one could object to that, unless one knows that some of the big brewers use far less. I have even heard of one big brewery which produces a drink for sale which contains no malted barley at all. Such things are not injurious to health, but should not be dignified with the name of beer.

3 The process of brewing

Malted barley is cracked by being passed through rollers, and the resultant 'grist' passes into a mash tun where it is held in hot water (about 150 degrees Fahrenheit) for around an hour. This 'mashing' converts the starch in the grain into sugars which dissolve into the water. The wort, as this sweet extract is called, is drawn off and the spent grains, which are of no further use for the brewer, can be sold off as cattle food.

The malt is now boiled up with hops for an hour or two in the copper, and modern brewers in Britain (with very rare exceptions, notably Guinness) add sugar. After about two hours the hopped wort is pumped into a vessel called the Hop Back, where the spent hops are filtered off, to be sold as fertilizer. The hopped wort is cooled and passed into the fermenting vessel where yeast is added. Fermentation lasts about six days, during which yeast turns the sugars into carbon dioxide and alcohol. The more sugars present in the original wort the higher the final quantity of alcohol. If the brewer allows all the sugar to be fermented then he will have what is called a fully attenuated beer: this will be strong but thin in flavour. If he stops the fermentation too early then he will have a rather sweet and not very strong beer. It is a matter of the brewer's skill and judgement to hit the right mean between these extremes.

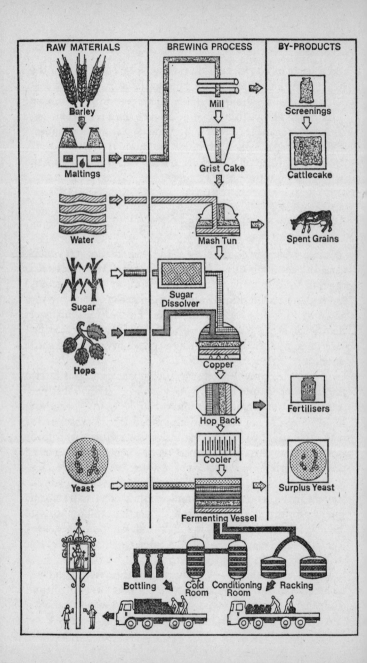

RAW MATERIALS	BREWING PROCESS	BY-PRODUCTS

Barley

Maltings

Water

Sugar

Hops

Yeast

Mill

Grist Cake

Mash Tun

Sugar Dissolver

Copper

Hop Back

Cooler

Fermenting Vessel

Screenings

Cattlecake

Spent Grains

Fertilisers

Surplus Yeast

Bottling Cold Room Conditioning Room Racking

When primary fermentation has been completed the beer (as it now is) is sometimes sugar-primed; then it is 'racked' into casks often containing a handful of dry hops. Traditional draught beer will also have finings added just before it leaves the brewery. The finings consist of isinglass, a substance made from the swim-bladders of sturgeons and other fish. The finings cause sediment to separate out, so that the beer is clear. This beer is still biologically alive, and a secondary fermentation will continue in the cask. Consequently it has to be treated with care and skill when it arrives at the pub, and once the cask is opened the beer will have to be consumed within a matter of days.

For bottled beers the usual procedure after fermentation is different. Instead of continuing to condition and remaining biologically alive up to the moment of consumption, bottled beer is generally clarified by filtration or centrifugation. Chilling and pasteurizing renders it stable (that is, dead). It is then restored to a semblance of life by being injected with carbon dioxide (CO_2), just like mineral waters and other fizzy drinks.

Bottled beer came in at the beginning of the century, but only really got going after the First World War. Because of the extra processes involved and the higher costs of transport and handling, bottled beer was more expensive than the traditional cask beer. Other than the price it had real advantages for the customer. Cask beer could be extremely unpleasant, especially if the publican was lazy or incompetent, or if the weather was thundery. It's worth remembering too that a great many publicans adulterated cask beer, either by pouring slops back into the barrel, or else by simply putting water into it. A retired exciseman has told me that between the wars it was reckoned that in London one publican in four watered the beer.

Bottled beer might cost more, but at least the customer had the satisfaction of getting beer in the condition in which it left the brewery. It was also clearer than draught beer, and was usually served in a fancier glass. Its success was rapid. By the beginning of the Second World War bottled beer accounted for about a third of the beer consumed, and by 1951 it was up to two-fifths. At present bottled and canned beers account for a little over a quarter.

4   Types of beer

Variations of materials and brewing techniques produce different kinds of beer. The most popular draught beer in Britain is bitter: the most under-rated is mild. During this century mild has declined sadly from its former eminence. Charrington's London brewery, for example, brewed only mild and stout at the beginning of this century. As late as 1929 bitter accounted for only 4 per cent of its output, but by 1968 the proportion had grown to 65 per cent. This was typical of what was happening nationally. In 1959 mild accounted for 42 per cent of the beer in the country. It is now down to about 13 per cent, and the decline shows no sign of halting. The brewers don't promote it, beer enthusiasts neglect it. The exception is the Midlands and the North-West, especially the Manchester area. Chester's brewery used to produce a delicious dark mild, so dark that the first time I went into a pub where it was being drunk I thought everyone was on draught Guinness. Regrettably Whitbread's have made Chester's 'Fighting' Mild into a 'bright' beer, gassed and filtered. However, the fortunate Mancunians still have plenty of splendid mild available. All the Manchester brewers produce mild, and Boddingtons', Hydes', J. W. Lees and Greenall Whitley all brew not one but two milds. Robinson's actually sell more mild than bitter. Hydes' ordinary mild sells about as much as the bitter, and their best mild about half as much.

Mild is brewed in the same way as bitter, but with darker malts, more sugar or caramel, and fewer hops. Its mildness is therefore a matter of flavour rather than alcoholic strength, though in practice mild is usually weaker than bitter. Mild is not a particularly precise term. Chester's Bitter for example (when it still existed) was darker than the mild of the nearby Robinson's brewery, while some Lancashire milds are so pale that to a southerner they look like bitter.

Old ale is a more powerful version of mild. It may be found under various names such as Winter Warmer, or Stock Ale. In the past it was often called Burton, but as it was not produced in that town the Trade Descriptions Act caused that name to disappear. Old ales are strong, and sometimes a little sweet. They are now only brewed by a few independent firms and often only in the winter. Examples include Wadworth's Old Timer, Brakspear's Old, Young's Winter Warmer, Harvey's Elizabethan, and Robinson's Old Tom.

The types of beer so far discussed can all be found in draught and bottled form. Pale Ale and Light Ale are usually a brewery's best bitter and ordinary bitter respectively, chilled, filtered, pasteurized, carbonated and bottled. Similarly Brown Ale is the bottled version of mild. The only stout that exists both in bottle and on draught is Guinness.

Guinness is one of the world's great drinks. This superb product owes its success not simply to the skill with which it has been advertised and promoted in the past half-century, but also to its own excellence. Its bitterness (especially that of bottled Guinness) may at first put off some people, but once acquired (usual time, half an hour) the taste for it is never lost. Many pubmen become exclusively Guinness drinkers and will touch nothing else. Outside Ireland the Guinness connoisseur usually drinks bottled Guinness, which is a living, naturally conditioned beer. In Great Britain draught Guinness is a keg beer: that is to say, it is delivered to the pubs in sealed casks from which it is expelled by the pressure of gas. The difference from other keg beers is that Guinness uses a mixture of CO_2 and nitrogen instead of just CO_2. Whether or not for this reason, draught Guinness does not have the unpleasant tingling gassiness of carbonated beers, but on the contrary is soft, foamy and smooth. Even the Guinness in tins is good, though it is not a living beer. But for the real draught Guinness you must go to Ireland where a glass of stout is poured with proper reverence. Draught Guinness in Ireland is still a naturally conditioned unpasteurized beer, and is sold in the living state, though it now arrives at the pub in a container known derogatorily as 'The Iron Lung'. In England a pint of Guinness is poured in about twenty seconds. In Ireland it may take five minutes or even (so I've heard) a quarter of an hour. In some Irish pubs it is well-advised to order your drink well in advance of need. A good Irish curate (barman) will pour a Guinness inch by inch, with great care, skill and affection. 'What a beautiful sight,' I murmured as such a glass was settling down one day in Dublin about three years ago. The inadequacy of my appreciation was brought home to me, in the nicest possible way, by Mr John Lombard, who was about to retire from the brewery after many years' service. He has a complete vocabulary and phraseology to describe the settling-out process of a glass of stout. Starting with the infinite darkness at the bottom of the glass ('Black is beautiful'), he worked up through the tumult of ascending and descending bubbles ('the phenomenon of surge'), pointing out the umbra and the penumbra, and so on all the way up to the meniscus at the top. It was rather like being taken round Chartres cathedral by Kenneth Clark.

If you look at a bottle of Guinness you will find that the label bears the words Extra Stout. This was to distinguish it from ordinary, or plain, stout. Plain, as it was known, or plain porter, was a weaker version, and existed in Ireland until only about four years ago. It bore to what we generally think of as Guinness the sort of relationship that mild

bears to bitter and, though now departed, achieved immortality in Flann O'Brien's glorious book *At Swim-Two-
Birds*:

The name or title of the pome I am about to recite,
gentlemen, said Shanahan with leisure priest-like in
character, is a pome by the name of the 'Workman's
Friend'. By God you can't beat it. I've heard it praised
by the highest. It's a pome about a thing that's known
to all of us. It's about a drink of porter . . . Now listen,
said Shanahan clearing the way with small coughs.
Listen now.

He arose holding his hand and bending his knee
beneath him on the chair.

> When things go wrong and will not come right,
> Though you do the best you can,
> When life looks black as the hour of night –
> A PINT OF PLAIN IS YOUR ONLY MAN.

By God there's a lilt in that, said Lamont.
Very good indeed, said Furriskey. Very nice.
I'm telling you it's the business, said Shanahan. Listen
now.

> When money's tight and is hard to get
> And your horse has also ran,
> When all you have is a heap of debt –
> A PINT OF PLAIN IS YOUR ONLY MAN.

> When health is bad and your heart feels strange,
> And your face is pale and wan,
> When doctors say that you need a change,
> A PINT OF PLAIN IS YOUR ONLY MAN.

> When food is scarce and your larder bare
> And no rashers grease your pan,
> When hunger grows as your meals are rare –
> A PINT OF PLAIN IS YOUR ONLY MAN.

What do you think of that now?

It's a pome that'll live, called Lamont, a pome that'll
be heard and clapped when plenty more . . .

But wait till you hear the last verse, man, the last
polish-off, said Shanahan. He frowned and waved his
hand.

Oh it's good, it's good, said Furriskey.

In time of trouble and lousy strife,
You have still got a darlint plan,
You still can turn to a brighter life –
A PINT OF PLAIN IS YOUR ONLY MAN!

Apart from Guinness there are a number of stouts which
have their following, but which are quite different because
they are not bitter. Mackeson is the best known of these,
but there are several others – Bass Charrington's Jubilee
Stout, Courage's Velvet Stout, Watney's Cream Label,
and various stouts brewed by regional breweries. One
on its own is Courage's very strong Russian Imperial
Stout, first brewed for the Empress Catherine of Russia
in the eighteenth century. Whereas most very strong beers
are fairly sweet, Russian Stout has an intriguing bitter-
sweet taste. The year of brewing appears on the bottle
label.

Barley wines are very strong bottled beers, the product
of a long maturing process, with a rich, usually sweet,
flavour. Most brewers make a barley wine. They are sold
in nip-sized bottles, and though their price is usually high
compared to that of other beer, in terms of alcohol they
are good value for money. One of these very strong beers
is roughly equivalent to a double whisky, at about half
the price.

The word *lager* comes from German *lagerbier*, meaning
store beer, beer kept in store. Real lager should be stored
for up to three months to allow it to condition. EKU
Urtyp, brewed in Kulmbach and said to be the strongest

beer in the world, is stored for nearly a year. Lager is normally fermented at a lower temperature than English beer, usually with a bottom-fermentation yeast.

In my experience the best lagers are brewed in Germany and Czechoslovakia, and at their best are superb. However, 80 per cent of the lager consumed in Britain is brewed here and much of it is feeble and characterless. The Teutonic-sounding names should mislead no one into thinking that these are imported drinks.

Between 1971 and 1974 sales of lager almost doubled. It now accounts for something like 18 per cent of the beer market, and some observers predict that by 1980 as much as a quarter of the beer drunk in Britain will be lager. Its success derives at least partly from extremely energetic promotion by the brewers, for whom it has the same advantages as keg beer (to be discussed later). In 1975 £1 million was spent on advertising Harp lager alone. Harp, with 20 per cent of the lager market, then the brand leader, is the product of Harp Lager Limited which was half owned by Guinness, quarter owned by Courage and quarter by Scottish and Newcastle, until early in 1975 when the proportions were minutely altered by the acquisition of two per cent by Greene King. Unlike authentic German lager, Harp contains maize flakes and caramel. Its main characteristic is a lack of characteristics. In May 1974 Michael Bateman wrote about Harp in the *Sunday Times*. 'What special characteristics make Harp the brand leader?' he asked one of its brewers, who innocently and revealingly replied, 'It's not so much what you can say for it. It's just that there's not much you can say against it.'

Perhaps as a reaction against the blandness of ordinary British-brewed lagers, demand has grown for stronger and more authentic lager, imported directly or brewed under licence from Denmark, Germany or Austria. Another growth sector has been Australian lager: many different Australian

brews are now available in Britain, and most are preferable
to the British lagers.

5   The quick and the dead

Most living beer comes in draught form: most bottled beer
is dead. However, to complicate things, some draught
beer (that is beer from a tap in a pub) is not alive, and some
bottled beer is. By far the best-known living bottled beer
is Guinness. It is a naturally conditioned beer, with a
secondary fermentation in the bottle, and with a sediment
that is concealed only by the intense darkness of the stout.
It is in peak condition about a fortnight after bottling, and
an important part of a publican's skill is making sure that
his Guinness stocks are rotating properly so that there are
no bottles left ageing at the back of the shelf. For the same
reason, it is best when buying Guinness for home consumption to buy enough for immediate needs rather than to
lay in a stock. It is also better (at least in my experience)
to buy Guinness at a pub than at an off-licence where the
bottle may have been sitting on the shelf for weeks.

The only other widely-available naturally conditioned
bottled beer is White Shield Worthington. This outstandingly delicious beer is now brewed by Bass Charrington
in Burton-on-Trent.

> Say, for what were hop-yards meant,
> Or why was Burton built on Trent?

The answer to the second part of A. E. Housman's question
is not that Burton's only there for the beer, but that it's
there for the water for the beer. Not the water of the Trent,
which is no more used for Burton's beer than (whatever
myth may say) Liffey water is used for Guinness. The water
for Burton's breweries comes from deep wells, and is full of
sulphates and carbonates of calcium and magnesium
(gypsum). This hard water is especially suitable for the

pale, bitter, highly-hopped beers for which Burton became famous in the eighteenth century, at a time when the London brewers were mainly brewing the dark stouts and milds which were suited to London's softer water. The most famous of Burton's many breweries were Worthington & Co., founded in 1744, and Bass & Co., founded in 1777 by a carrier called William Bass, who sold his business to another firm of carriers called Pickford's and took to brewing instead, greatly to the benefit of mankind.

White Shield, like some other of Bass Worthington's beers, is still brewed by the Burton Union system, so called because it is unique to Burton and because much of the fermentation takes place in large wooden casks called Unions (precisely how much a Union holds was a matter on which Bass and Worthington differed: since they are now the same firm it is not a matter of great importance, though not necessarily less interesting for that). At the Bass Worthington brewery there is an enormous hall full of these Union casks from which the yeast is constantly foaming out through the spigot hole, up swan-neck pipes and into a trough. As well as being a magnificent sight, the Union system has two clear advantages. One is that the yeast enjoys it enormously – so much so that the same batch has been going for a century and a half and looks in good shape for another 150 years. The other is that it makes excellent beer – draught Bass, Bass barley wine, Worthington BB, Continental Bass (a strong beer sold abroad) and White Shield Worthington.

White Shield is quite strong (original gravity of 1053 degrees) but not so strong as to have the sweetness that spoils many barley wines and other strong beers. It has a distinctive, dry flavour that is often described as nutty, and it's one of the world's great beers. In this case virtue is being rewarded: at a time when there has been a general trading down to cheaper beers, sales of White Shield in 1975 were 17 per cent up on the previous year.

Like many good things, it requires, and rewards, a little trouble. When it arrives at your pub or home it should be kept in a cool room (54 to 58 degrees) for four days to let the sediment settle. It should be in prime condition for drinking around four weeks after bottling, the date of which is easily discovered once you know the coding system, which I shall now explain. You will find printed in the middle of the label a numeral from 1 to 13. On the right hand edge of the label there will be one, two, three or four tiny nicks torn into the paper. The number of these tears indicates the quarter of the year in which the beer was bottled; the numeral in the middle of the label denotes the week of the quarter. Thus a bottle label with two nicks and the number 13 means the beer was bottled in the thirteenth week of the second quarter, that is to say the last week of June. It will be in prime condition about four weeks later, and will stay in condition for as much as nine months, after which it may develop a sulphury taste as it goes out of condition. If, however, you keep it for as long as fifteen months one of two things may happen. If you are very unlucky it will develop a really unpleasant flavour. Most bottles, however, should come back into condition with a flavour that is different from the original but which some connoisseurs consider to be even better.

There are barmaids who burst into tears when asked to pour a White Shield, but it's not really all that difficult. First, remove the crown cap, preferably moving the opener while keeping the bottle stationary so as to avoid disturbing the sediment. Start pouring, keeping glass and bottle at eye level. As the glass fills, raise the bottle slightly, so that the fall will produce a good head, but don't do this too soon or you won't get it all in the glass. At the same time as you're making sure that none spills and that the head is coming on nicely, you must be keeping an eye on the sediment. As soon as this starts creeping up the neck of the bottle, stop pouring. You should now have a glass of star-bright beer with a head that stands proud of the glass but does not overflow. There are additional refinements, like not letting the bottle touch the glass, and holding the bottle so that the label is clearly visible to your customer or friend, but that is in broad outline approximately how to pour a White Shield.

Drinking is carried out in the normal way, by raising the glass to the slightly parted lips, pouring the liquid into the mouth and then swallowing it, again making sure that there is no spillage. The next step is the one over which opinion is sharply divided. The following is my own practice, for what it is worth. Having poured the beer with immense care to prevent any sediment entering the glass and having drunk an inch or two, give the bottle a good shake and *pour the sediment from the bottle into the glass*.

There are a number of reasons for doing this. First of all, by making the careful pouring pointless, it establishes that the pouring of a White Shield is an activity, a skill, perhaps even an art, in itself, needing no prosaic functional purpose for its justification.

Second, it causes consternation in the pub. The barmaid who has so far bravely held back her tears may now release them in a flood. The landlord may threaten to throw you out. Customers who have not spoken to one another for years – customers who have not spoken to anyone for years – suddenly become animated and loquacious. There is no better way of livening up a sleepy pub.

Third, it tastes good, and does you good. Yeast has all sorts of beneficial effects. It is because they drink yeasty beer that brewery workers live to such advanced ages: I wouldn't be surprised if there are breweries with more retired than active members of the staff. Running a brewery pension fund must be a nightmare; they have to keep paying out for such a long time.

Incidentally in Australia the naturally-conditioned sediment beer of Cooper & Sons of Adelaide is usually shaken well before being poured, and a good cloudy glassful is considered something to be proud of.

Apart from Guinness and White Shield Worthington, only a few other naturally-conditioned bottled beers with sediment are available. They are Courage's Russian Imperial Stout; Gale's Prize Old Ale, a remarkable beer, reddish in colour, and the only British bottled beer still closed with a cork; Eldridge Pope's Thomas Hardy Ale (brewed only very rarely); Chimay, brewed in silence by Trappist monks at the Abbey of Notre Dame de Scourmont at Chimay, Belgium, and available from a few off-licences; and, of course, all home-brewed beer in bottles.

DRAUGHT

We have seen that not all bottled beer is dead: nor is all draught beer alive. 'Keg' beer is treated like most bottled beer; chilled, filtered, pasteurized, carbonated and put into pressurized containers from which it is delivered by the pressure of carbon dioxide. Since it never makes contact with the air and since it is completely stable (the stability of lifelessness), it is entirely consistent in quality. Unlike traditional draught beer it does not have to be sold quickly once opened. It is therefore very suitable for clubs and other places with fluctuating sales – very busy after the rugby game on Saturday, for example, almost nothing for the rest of the week. It also has the real advantage of needing no skill on the part of the barman, and good barmen are not easy to find. Its disadvantages, at least for those with a taste for traditional English beer, are that it is usually sweet and full of gas.

Keg beers have been vigorously promoted by the big brewers. The best-known are Allied's Double Diamond, Courage's Tavern, Bass Charrington's Worthington E, Scottish and Newcastle's Tartan, Watney's Red and Whitbread's Tankard. There's little to choose between them, and personally I don't care for any of them.

The distinction made so far has been between living beer and dead, either of which can come in bottled or draught form. We now come to the rather complicated question of the means of dispensing draught beer. In order to serve traditional English draught beer the publican knocks a tap into the bung-hole at the end, and allows air into the cask through what is called the spile-hole at the top. He then merely turns the tap and gravity shifts the beer from the cask into your glass, where it is needed. Alternatively, the cask can stay in the cellar, attached to a beer-engine which pumps up the beer by means of the familiar truncheon-shaped pump-handle. In some parts of the country, especially the Midlands and the North, the hand pumps have generally been replaced by electric pumps. These should not be confused with the bar-mounted chromium taps of the keg beers or top-pressure systems.

Top-pressure is something of a hybrid. It is usually a traditionally brewed, naturally conditioned beer, but is dispensed by CO_2 pressure after the manner of keg beer. For the brewer and publican this has the advantage that the beer never comes in contact with the atmosphere and that it therefore keeps much better, being free from airborne infections. Some consumers, on the other hand, claim that the carbon dioxide enters the beer and makes it gassy.

Controversy continues to rage on this subject. It is worth bearing in mind that beer is very difficult to carbonate and when this is done deliberately (as with keg and bottled beer), the pressure required is considerably higher than that used by top-pressure systems. In practice it seems to depend on the beer, the conditions and the cellarman. If the cellar is deep the pressure required to raise it is higher; if it is kept at this high pressure all through the night when not in use, it can become as fizzy as keg beer. On the other hand there are some systems which merely use a blanket of CO_2

on top of the beer to keep it from contamination, and use a pump to move the beer from cellar to glass. This seems to me acceptable both in theory and practice, but would not meet the approval of the more doctrinaire members of Camra who have at times shown the fanaticism of religious dementia on this subject. They consider anything that in any way uses extraneous CO_2 to be non-kosher. This can involve questions of an almost philosophical nature, since a living beer is giving out carbon dioxide of its own the whole time. Camra's annual general meeting in 1975 even passed a motion expressing an objection to electric pumps. At times it has seemed that Camra's sole interest was in means of dispense. It has been said that some of their members would drink castor oil if it came from a hand pump, and would reject nectar if it had no more than looked at carbon dioxide. Naturally they are at liberty to entertain whatever notions, and carry whatever motions, they like, but they have often denied themselves excellent beer in the process. Top-pressure beer can be fizzy, it can be delicious. Hand-pumped beer can be delicious, it can be revolting. The deciding factor must be the experience of drinking the beer, and not the rigid application of doctrinaire requirements.

6 Strength

In the United Kingdom the alcoholic strength of beer is indicated by, and excise duty is charged on, original gravity (o.g.). This is the specific gravity of the wort before it has started to ferment. If the specific gravity of water is expressed as 1000 degrees, anything above that figure in the specific gravity of the wort will indicate the quantity of malt and sugars present. When the yeast is added and fermentation begins, the sugars are turned into alcohol and carbon dioxide, and the specific gravity drops. The further it drops, the more alcohol there is. Usually the brewer stops fermentation when the gravity is about a quarter to a fifth of the original gravity. The percentage of alcohol by weight is about a tenth of the drop. Thus for example a beer with an o.g. of 1040 and a final gravity (sometimes called present gravity) of 1010 will contain about 3 per cent alcohol. Knowing the original gravity therefore does not tell you the precise strength, but gives you some indication of it.

For a long time the only brewery in the country publicly to declare the o.g. of its beers was the Northern Clubs' Federation Brewery, whose Federation Special Ale, as supplied to the House of Commons, has an original gravity of 1041. In 1974 Young's of Wandsworth and Ruddle's of Rutland followed suit and published their original gravities, and in 1975 Higson's of Liverpool did likewise. Large supermarket chains such as Sainsbury's and Marks and Spencer also declared the strength of their 'own brand' beers. Thus Marks and Spencer declare their Yorkshire Strong Brown Ale as 1050 o.g., 4·75 per cent alcohol by volume, and Sainsbury's label their canned Pale Ale (brewed by Ruddle's) as 3·5 per cent alcohol by volume.

The other brewers, especially the big ones, maintained a coy silence on the subject of alcoholic content. They gave various reasons, often self-contradictory, for their reticence. They said that original gravity is not an indication of flavour: this is true but irrelevant. They said that beer is not a drink that people consume in order to get drunk – although their advertisements either explicitly or by suggestion are always emphasizing the strength of beer. They also boasted that beer is virtually as strong now as it was 20 years ago. The average o.g. for all beer in 1952 was 1037·07 and in 1972 was 1036·88. This comparison conveniently ignores the decline in the consumption of mild, which in the same period dropped from nearly half of all beer sales to less than a quarter. Since mild is generally weaker than bitter, it follows as the night the day that if the average for all beer has stayed the same then the strength of bitter must have declined. Which it has. The decline is even more pronounced if one takes a longer time scale. In 1900 the average o.g. was 1055, and in 1880 1057. Here are the average gravities of British beer at five-yearly intervals for the last half-century:

1923	1042·72
1928	1043·17
1933	1039·52
1938	1041·02
1943	1034·34
1948	1032·66
1953	1036·87
1958	1037·48
1963	1037·70
1968	1037·36
1973	1036·99

The brewers are possibly right in saying that people don't want the strong beers of the beginning of the century (though this is not confirmed by the enormous increase in popularity of strong draught beers such as Young's Winter Warmer, Wadworth's Old Timer, Fuller, Smith and Turner's Extra Special Bitter and Ruddle's County). But none of this is an argument for not giving us some indication of the strength of what we are buying. Anyway, in due course the brewers will be forced by EEC regulations to work out some kind of banding system which will indicate whether a beer is strong, medium or weak.

At present beer is not controlled by the labelling of food regulations and it should be. Beer is taxed according to strength and the customer has a right to know what he is getting for his money. In February 1975 Mr Ernest Underwood, public analyst for South Yorkshire, reported the results of tests he had made on 44 different types of beer. He found that brown ale varied in alcohol content from 2·7 per cent to 4·58 per cent; light ale from 2·99 to 3·94; pale ale from 2·99 to 4·66; lager from 2·5 to 8·47; barley wine from 8·3 to 11·9; stout from 4·58 to 4·73; and the rest (including bitter) from 2·7 to 6·56. He found little relationship between alcoholic content and price.

While there are no good reasons for keeping this information from us there are plenty why it should be given. It could be important for a diabetic, for example, or for a motorist drinking a beer he is unfamiliar with. When we buy tinned food, the label tells us what we are paying for. The law protects us from dairies which water their milk, and publicans can be prosecuted for watering the beer, but the brewer is under no obligation to tell us what his beer is made of or how much water it contains.

The policy of not disclosing original gravities first took a knock from independent analyses by various people, outside the industry, and now seems to be collapsing entirely. Camra's 1976 *Good Beer Guide* publishes the original gravity of all draught beer in Britain, much of this information having come from the brewers themselves. This is a complete turnabout. The figures show that the beers of the independent regional breweries are consistently stronger than those of the big brewers, and of course cheaper. The following are the strengths of the much-promoted keg beers of the Big Six national brewers:

	Original Gravity	% *alcohol*
Double Diamond (Allied Breweries)	1037·8	3·5
Keg Worthington E (Bass Charrington)	1039·1	4·2
Courage Tavern	1038·0	3·8
Younger's Tartan (Scottish and Newcastle)	1035·9	3·9
Watney's Red	1037·8	3·4
Whitbread Tankard	1038·5	3·9

(source: *What's Brewing*, journal of CAMRA)

The following are some strong beers:

Fuller's ESB	1055·8
Ruddle's County	1050
Young's Special	1047
Brakspear's Special	1042·35
Courage Directors	1048
Greene King Abbot	1048
Bottled Guinness	1045 in winter, 1042 in summer
Newcastle Brown	1047

It is worth noting that Fuller's ESB, the strongest bitter in Britain, would have been below average strength in 1900.

I should emphasize that I am not taking alcoholic strength as a standard by which to judge beer. There are many delicious milds that are much weaker than the keg beers mentioned above, and one of the best-tasting beers in the country, King and Barnes bitter, has an o.g. of under 1035. Strong beers are often rather sweet and for this reason I personally prefer Brakspear's ordinary bitter, for example, to its Special, and Young's ordinary to its Special.

The very strongest beers are bottled. EKU Urtyp is claimed to be the strongest beer in the world at 1117·6 o.g., 13·2 per cent alcohol by volume, which makes it stronger than most wine. The strongest regularly brewed British beer is Courage's Russian Stout, which is brewed once a year and usually comes out at around 1100 (10·2 per cent alcohol). Whitbread Gold Label is the most widely available strong beer at about 1100 (10·6 per cent). In fact the strongest beer brewed anywhere, but only occasionally, is Eldridge Pope's Thomas Hardy Ale at 1120; the brewery recommend that it should be kept for four years before drinking, but the brewery's managing director, Mr Christopher Pope, tells me that ten years would probably be 'much more satisfactory'. The name of the beer is a tribute to Hardy's description of the beer of Casterbridge (that is Dorchester, where the Eldridge Pope brewery is to be found) in *The Trumpet Major*:

It was of the most beautiful colour that the eye of an
artist in beer could desire; full in body, yet brisk as a
volcano; piquant, yet without a twang; luminous as an
autumn sunset; free from streakiness of taste; but,
finally, rather heady. The masses worshipped it, the
minor gentry loved it more than wine, and by the most
illustrious county families it was not despised. Anybody
brought up for being drunk and disorderly in the streets
of its natal borough, had only to prove that he was a
stranger to the place and its liquor to be honourably
dismissed by the magistrates, as one overtaken in a fault
that no man could guard against who entered the town
unawares.

After reading that it is going to be extremely difficult to
wait until 1978 to open my bottle – let alone 1984.

7 Temperature – some like it warm

In the long hot summer of 1975 a German civil servant and
lover of horses called Dr Heinrich Bekaan celebrated the
birth of a foal to his mare by giving a barbecue party.
At the appointed hour the sausages were ready and the beer
was cool and straight from the fridge. Unfortunately the
guests were all late and by the time they arrived the
bangers were black and the beer was warm. They added
insult to injury by making such pointed remarks on the
subject that the Herr Doktor retired, returning shortly
with his shotgun. On finding that his ungrateful guests
were still complaining, he opened fire and in no time
thirteen of his friends were stretched out on the ground.
None suffered worse than superficial wounds to the arms
and legs, but even so Dr Bekaan was suspended from his
parliamentary duties.

Personally I like my bangers well done and would not

have earned a place at the end of Dr Bekaan's gun-sights on that score. The temperature of the beer is another matter. Presumably the beer concerned was lager, which does want to be fairly cold. If the trigger-happy host had been serving traditional English beer none of this need have happened, as may be illustrated by another story, this time by James Joyce. In 'Ivy Day in the Committee Room' in *Dubliners*, a group of men find themselves with some bottles of stout but no corkscrew (in Ireland Guinness came in corked bottles until quite recently). Mr Henchy solves this problem by putting the bottles close to the fire, and 'In a few minutes an apologetic "Pok!" was heard as the cork flew out of Mr Lyon's bottle.'

In order to expel the cork the contents of the bottle must have reached a fair temperature and were doubtless none the worse for it. Far better a bottle of Guinness warmed by the fire than frozen in the fridge, as is the tendency in our decadent times.

The ideal temperature at which to serve beer is closely related to the one at which it is brewed. Lager should therefore be about 45–50 degrees F (7–10 degrees C). Inferior lager and keg beers may be served at much lower temperatures, since this effectively disguises the flavour. Top-fermented British beer should be served at just below room temperature, 55–60 degrees F. In winter it is very pleasant to have much warmer beer in the form of mulled ale, wassails, and punches. Recipes will be found on pages 123–5.

IV Modern Times

In 1881 there were more than 16,000 brewing companies in the United Kingdom. There are now fewer than a hundred. The process of concentration in the structure of the industry took place first in London, where by the beginning of the nineteenth century the supply of beer was dominated by a dozen large brewers. With their greater skill, steam power and more reliable product the big firms displaced brewing both in the pub and in the home. At first London was a special case: in 1830 seventeen pubs in London brewed their own beer; in the rest of the country there were 23,572. In the course of the century this domination of the industry by the big businesses gradually became national. In an interesting book about beer published in 1886, John Bickerdyke laments that 'Not only has the practice of domestic brewing much declined, but from the same causes there has been of late years an extraordinary and lamentable decrease in the numbers of small country brewers.'

The entanglements of Gladstone's Inland Revenue Act of 1880, reinforced by the shortages of two world wars, had virtually eradicated domestic brewing by the middle of this century. Pubs brewing their own beer also diminished in number: 12,417 in 1880; 1,447 in 1914; 7 in 1966; 4 in 1974. Gone too are the days when every sizeable town had three or four breweries, and even quite small villages would sometimes have one. The table below shows how throughout this century breweries have become ever fewer and bigger:

Year	Brewer-for-sale licences	Average output per brewery (in thousands of barrels)
1900	6,447 (including Republic of Ireland)	5·5
1910	4,512	8·0
1920	2,914	12·0
1930	1,418 (not including Republic of Ireland)	15·5
1940	840	30·0
1950	567	46·0
1960	358	73·4
1968	211	146·0
1973	162	217·0 (estimate)

A table giving the numbers of brewing companies (as opposed to breweries) would show the same decline – from 859 in 1923 to 87 in 1973. Even these diminishing figures conceal the full extent of the move towards monopoly, since three-quarters of the beer in Britain is produced by a mere seven companies. These are Allied Breweries, Bass Charrington, Courage, Scottish and Newcastle, Watney Mann, Whitbread's and Guinness. (References to the 'Big Six' rather than the 'Big Seven' exclude Guinness as a special case, since this company owns no pubs.)

Some of the reasons for the reduction in the number of breweries and brewing companies have been perfectly sensible. Not all of the small breweries were competently run, and some of them produced truly awful beer. Some fell victim to death duties, but in many cases they were useful, economically profitable units which were simply gobbled up by their bigger expansionist neighbours. It was soon found that, because of the tied house system, buying up brewing companies was a cheap way of buying pubs and thereby increasing the number of guaranteed retail outlets: as for the breweries themselves, these could be closed down and used as bottling plants or simply sold off for property development.

As well as mopping up the small fry there were many amalgamations between the big companies themselves. Bass and Worthington, the two brewers which had made Burton-on-Trent famous all over the world, merged in 1927. Barclay, Perkins bought Style and Winch in 1929. After a temporary interruption during the war years of 1939 to 1945, the process accelerated in the 1960s when various outsiders tried to break into the exclusive circles of what was known as 'the beerage'. A Canadian by the name of E. P. Taylor, who had visions of the whole world drinking Carling lager, came and went in the 1960s, leaving in his wake the Bass Charrington conglomerate, the largest brewing business in Europe with more than 10,000 pubs, hotels and off-licences. It was formed in 1967 out of the merger of Bass, Mitchells and Butlers with Charrington United Breweries. These were themselves the product of mergers: Bass and Worthington merged with Mitchells and Butlers in 1961; Charrington merged with United Breweries of York in 1962 to form Charrington United Breweries.

The property developer Charles Clore's attempt to buy Watney's in the 1960s was unsuccessful, but it was a near enough miss to scare the big brewers into further huddling together in the hope of continuing to exclude non-members of the beerage. They failed. Watney's escaped the clutches of Charles Clore only to fall into the hands of Maxwell Joseph; in the biggest takeover ever, Grand Metropolitan paid £413 million for Watney's. Likewise Courage, after endless mergers which might have been expected to ensure its independence, ended up by being bought by a firm of cigarette manufacturers.

The cannibalistic way in which the Big Six developed reminds one of W. S. Gilbert's 'The Yarn of the "Nancy Bell"', in which the starving crew are reduced to eating one of their number, and then another, and then another, until the entire crew is incorporated in a single survivor:

> Oh, I am a cook and a captain bold,
>> And the mate of the *Nancy* brig,
> And a bo'sun tight, and a midshipmite,
>> And the crew of the captain's gig.

The fortunes of the Reading brewing company, H. and G. Simonds, may serve as a paradigm of the way the British brewing industry developed in this century (many other examples would serve just as well.) The success of the brewery that William Blackall Simonds founded in Reading in 1774 owed much to the fact that one of its biggest customers was the British Army. Early in this century H. and G. Simonds started acquiring other brewing companies and to grow bigger and bigger. These are some of the companies they bought:

1919	Tamar Brewery, Devonport
1920	South Berkshire Brewery, Newbury (which had itself taken over Blandy Hawkins of Reading)
1925	Plough Brewery, Wandsworth
1930	Ashby's Staines Brewery with its subsidiary Wheelers Wycombe of High Wycombe, which had itself taken over Harris's Knowle Green Brewery at Staines in 1903
1931	The Newbury Brewery
1935	W. Rogers, Bristol
1937	Lakeman's, Brixham
1937	Cirencester Brewery
1938	R. H. Stiles, Bridgend
1939	J. L. Marsh, Blandford Forum
1945	R. B. Bowly, Swindon
1947	John May, Basingstoke
1949	Phillips & Sons, Newport

1950   R. Grant & Sons of Torquay (wine and spirits)

1954   Octagon Brewery, Plymouth.

Having swallowed a great many little fish, H. and G. Simonds had now become a big fish with around 1,500 licensed properties and assets worth over £10 million. Then an even bigger fish came along. Courage had merged with Barclay Perkins in 1955 to form Courage & Barclay. In 1960 this company acquired the ordinary share capital of H. and G. Simonds Ltd, thereby forming Courage Barclay & Simonds. To this assemblage were added George's of Bristol in 1961, John Smith's of Tadcaster in 1970 and Plymouth Breweries in 1971. Finally in 1972 Courage's Ltd (as it was now called – Barclay, Perkins, Simonds and other great brewing names having been dropped down the memory hole) was bought by the Imperial Tobacco Company (now called the Imperial Group, which at least sounds healthier).

Similar trails have been followed by the other big brewing companies. Watney Mann was the result of a merger by Watney, Combe and Reid with Mann, Crossman and Paulin in 1958. Somewhere in this great combine disappeared Tamplin's, Bullard's, Steward and Patteson, Phipps, and many others. Watney Mann was itself then acquired by Grand Met, which already owned Truman's. By now concern was being expressed about the slide towards monopoly, and on behalf of Grand Metropolitan Hotels Mr Maxwell Joseph went to great pains to allay such fears. On the first page of his offer document of 13 April 1972, he stated that 'it will be our policy to allow the brewing businesses of Watney and Truman to continue as separate and autonomous units.' In the revised offer document of 31 May 1972, Mr Joseph reiterated that 'no rationalization of the activities of Watney and Truman will take place in the short term and the autonomy of the two companies will be preserved.' On those terms his bid was successful.

In spite of these repeated undertakings, a little more than a year later Grand Met announced that Watney Mann and Truman were to be merged into a single 'profit centre'.

Allied Breweries came into being in 1961 as the result of a merger between Ind Coope, Tetley Walker and Ansells, making it the second biggest beer producer in Britain, with some 8,000 pubs as well. Scottish Brewers (including Younger's and McEwan's) merged with the Newcastle Breweries in 1960 to form Scottish and Newcastle.

Whitbread's followed a different route, by means of a device called the Whitbread umbrella. This was a benevolent-looking arrangement of 'association' rather than amalgamation or takeover which was supposed to preserve the smaller company's identity and independence while giving it financial stability and protecting it from marauding big brewers who were going about swallowing the little ones up. In the event, it turned out a bit like the story of the mice who hired a cat to protect them from the fierce creature they heard miaowing at night. Many went in under the shelter of the Whitbread umbrella never to emerge again. Such firms as Tomson and Wotton, Lacon's, and Nimmo's, have disappeared without trace, and others like Brickwood's, Strong of Romsey, Fremlin's, Threlfall's, Flower's and Tennant's exist in hardly more than name. Whitbread's cleverly fostered an image of benevolence, but the fact is that between 1960 and 1971 Whitbread's closed down fifteen breweries. Nor did the umbrella inhibit the company from the straight takeover. In 1968, the year in which the Monopolies Commission was gathering evidence for its report on the supply of beer, eight brewing companies in the country were taken over, five of them by Whitbread's: Bentley's Yorkshire Breweries, Cobb & Co., Tomson & Wotton, Whitaker, Richards & Sons, and John Young & Co. (not to be confused with the still happily and proudly independent Young & Co. of Wandsworth).

The big brewers should not be cast in the role of unmitigated villains. In the 1950s and early 1960s many small brewers were only too happy to sell up. Apart from the hammer-blows of death duties there was the general problem that the industry as a whole was in decline. Beer consumption dropped from 33 million barrels in 1946 to around 25 million barrels a year throughout the 1950s. The pubs of that time had a certain appeal to those with Graham Greene's taste for the seedy, but for a diminishing number of other people. Television was another factor keeping people at home and out of the pubs. For many small brewers the temptation to cut their losses was not one they could resist.

Therefore some degree of concentration in the brewing industry was inevitable and even desirable, but the process gathered such momentum that it became an end in itself. True to the spirit of the age the brewers joined in the worship of sheer size. They succumbed without resistance to the disease that E. F. Schumacher has called giantism.

Perhaps in the mid-1970s it is no longer assumed quite so unquestioningly as it used to be that bigger must mean better, that size is in itself desirable, but too often the disease reached such an advanced stage that last-minute doubts came too late to check it. As far as the brewing industry is concerned, the move to monopoly went so far that, even if it has now slowed down, it caused considerable damage to the industry and to the interests of consumers.

Bigger units are more efficient: that this belief was at least simplistic, and possibly simple-minded as well, was always obvious to all with eyes to see, but it was enough to maintain our captains of industry for many years. The phrase 'economies of scale', though not very big, was sufficient to crowd their minds, and having latched on to something approaching an idea they clung to it with a tenacity more admirable in a rat-catcher's dog than in those responsible for shaping our economy and society. Giantism raged unchecked in the 1950s and 1960s, infecting almost every aspect of our society from architecture to education, and nowhere more so than in the brewing industry.

The theory of the division of labour, and the example of mass production and the assembly line, had shown that in specific situations economies could be achieved by working on a bigger scale. The brewers were among those who extrapolated from this towards the huge, unjustified and dangerous generalization that in all situations bigger scale means more efficiency and higher profits. As long ago as 1929 the *Brewery Manual* was confidently stating that 'It has been found from experience that larger units in the brewery trade mean a substantial saving in working expenses and overhead charges.' Professor John Vaizey's study of the British brewing industry, published in 1960, has as its consistent underlying theme that the only future for the brewing industry is in big units. Professor Vaizey's book is factually valuable, but what makes it so fascinating to read fifteen years later is the sheer wrongness of his analysis. (The best sentence in the book reads: 'Attempts to sell continental-style lager have failed.' Lager now represents about 18 per cent of the market and is still growing fast).

At the time when Professor Vaizey was writing there were still 540 breweries being operated by some 310 companies, and about one-third of the beer was produced by 52 large firms. Enthusiastically he lists the factors operating to reduce the number of small breweries still further:

The first is the low prime costs associated with brewing to capacity of vessels, and of the organization. The capacity of these vessels is above that of the very small breweries, but even so it is still sufficiently low to allow breweries of 60,000 barrels output a year, or even less, to brew to capacity, and so achieve economies. But, secondly, the use of additional capital to lower the whole marginal cost curve can make a significant difference in the long run, and technological change has been on the side of the bigger breweries. The greater use of ancillary capital enables them to brew more efficiently, and so reduce waste, particularly from spoiled beer, and to increase the extraction rate from raw materials, thus reducing material costs. It enables them to brew beer which is more specifically suited to the markets which they were serving, or wish to break into.

Professor Vaizey calculated that for a brewery to be viable it must produce a minimum of 50–60,000 barrels a year. As we shall see, things have turned out rather differently. Here let it just be said that the breweries that are doing conspicuously well at the moment are small breweries like Ruddle's and Brakspear's producing about 30,000 barrels a year. In 1974 the sale of beer as a whole increased by ·89 per cent. Against this national figure comparatively small, regional producers of traditional beer have been reporting increases of sales of over 100 per cent. Not only do more and more customers find the beer of such firms – alphabetically from Adnams of Southwold to Young's of Wandsworth – a better product: it also costs less. The supposed 'economies of scale' obstinately refuse to show themselves in terms of retail price. The traditional beers of the theoretically inefficient small brewers are consistently cheaper than the products of gleaming new breweries producing 2 million barrels a year.

These giants, which have only recently come into operation, were planned many years ago as a result of the kind of thinking represented by Professor Vaizey's book. An important factor was transport. Beer is a bulky product, consisting mostly of water, and in the past has had a limited life. Until the end of the eighteenth century it was therefore uneconomic to produce beer far from the point of consumption. The London brewers were able to become big because they were in an area of high population: they remained local rather than national. With the development

first of rail and then of an efficient road system and motor
transport, the situation changed. Transport became faster
and cheaper, and as the duty on beer constantly rose,
transport costs became proportionately smaller.

To brewers and economists of Professor Vaizey's way
of thinking this all pointed to an obvious strategy: close
down the antiquated small breweries that were scattered
about the country and build a few huge breweries to serve
the entire country, with cheap transport, national marketing
and advertising and all the other advantages of being big
and strong.

Though the cost of transport no longer required a brewery
to be close to the point of sale, there was still the problem
of the limited life of beer. The answer was to have beer
which did not have a limited life. This meant the 'stable'
(i.e. dead) beers – bottled, canned, keg and lager. They
kept well, were consistent in quality and did not require
skilled staff to serve them. The higher price of keg beer did
not seem to worry the increasingly affluent customers of
the 1960s. Young people especially seemed to like them
(perhaps because of their sweetness) and not only were
young people the ones with money in their pockets and time
to spend it, but also they were the drinkers of tomorrow.

The strategy was thus to close down small local breweries
producing varied and variable traditional beers, and
replace them with vast centralized breweries producing a
national product. Millions of pounds of advertising every
year were lavished on advertising the keg beers: Allied's
Double Diamond, Courage's Tavern, Keg Worthington E,
Younger's Tartan, Watney's Red and Whitbread's Tankard. So confident were the big companies in the future of
these beers (and in the demise of traditional draught beer)
that some put, so to speak, all their kegs in one basket.
Watney's gave up traditional beer altogether, concentrating
solely on the keg Watney's Red and the container Special.
Throughout the 1960s, in pubs all over the country, the

old hand pumps were falling into disuse or being removed altogether and replaced by chromium-mounted taps with garish illuminated bar fittings. The familiar truncheon-shaped handles were becoming non-functional parts of the decor.

Local brews became fewer every year. Big companies bought up local ones. Sometimes the brewery was simply closed down. The local beer would be on sale one day and the next would simply be replaced by a national product. Sometimes it was done more subtly.

In the 1950s Watney's took over Tamplin's of Brighton and Henty & Constable of Chichester. The quite different draught bitters of these two companies ceased to be brewed and were replaced by 'Sussex Bitter', which was not as good as either of them, though preferable to Watney's national beers. Gradually, however, Sussex Bitter was run down and replaced by Watney's Special which in 1970 replaced Sussex Bitter altogether. A similar course appears to have been emerging in East Anglia with the Norwich Bitter which replaced those of Bullard's brewery and Steward & Patteson's, companies which Watney's took over in 1963.

Such examples were part of a large and complex operation which would be wearisome to follow in detail. The upshot was that the big brewing companies were fast moving towards monopoly, that the choice of beer was rapidly diminishing, and that it was becoming increasingly difficult in most parts of the country to buy traditional draught beer served without excessive carbonation. In retrospect, it is surprising that such complaints as were heard in the 1960s were more about what was being done to pubs than beer. The vandalizing of city and country pubs was so visibly and audibly offensive that to some extent it concealed what was being done more covertly to the beer. A few seasoned drinkers registered plaintive burps, belches and other minor explosions of the digestive tract, but the opinion of these old duffers was of small account in the swinging sixties' atmosphere of what Christopher Booker has called *neophilia*, the love of the new.

Everything was going swimmingly for the big brewers, and some of the more go-ahead of the small ones were following their example and might just survive. As for the die-hard, stick-in-the-mud traditionalists, they would soon be out of business. If traditional beer was to survive it would only be here and there in small pockets as a quaint reminder of Merrie England, like Beefeaters or horse-drawn ploughs, or the roasted ox on the village green. The chairman of one independent brewery that never budged from traditional beer remembers the mingled pity and contempt with which he used to be treated by his counterparts from the bigger companies in the Brewers' Society. 'Poor old so-and-so,' one of them used to say, 'every time he sees a funeral go by he must think "There goes another of my customers".'

The position of the big brewers appeared impregnable. They were so large and powerful that they operated like the massive national and international corporations that John Kenneth Galbraith describes in *The New Industrial State*. These companies act in ways which are different not just in scale but in kind from the competing, local business firms of conventional market economies. Galbraith argues that, instead of responding to the demands of the market, these large corporations on the contrary accommodate the consumer to their needs. Instead of producing what people are asking for they come up with something that is convenient for them to produce and then, with the help of massive advertising and sophisticated sales techniques, create a demand for it. What enables them to do this (unlike the small manufacturer) is the sheer quantity of their production, which establishes the norm and thereby sets the fashion. Galbraith points out that since General Motors makes about half the cars in the United States its designs do not reflect the current mode, they *are* the current mode. 'The proper shape of an automobile, for most people, will be what the automobile majors decree the current shape to be.'

Since it is less trouble to make a few products than many, the big companies increase standardization and, while continuing to announce that they are only supplying what the market demands, they in fact reduce the choice. Whereas fifty years ago hundreds of medium-sized companies might between them have been making thousands of different products, nowadays half-a-dozen vast companies will between them be making hundreds, perhaps tens, of almost identical products.

This analysis is still not widely accepted by the conventional wisdom, and the defenders of big business and the believers in centralized mass-production still claim that they are subject to market forces like everyone else. And so they would be, if the consumers were in a position to revolt.

Galbraith's argument is beautifully illustrated by the example of the British brewing industry in the past ten to twenty years. The big companies, in the very act of growing big, reduced the customer's choice by taking over and closing down smaller local breweries. This process has continued as they have centralized their operations and closed down their own local and even regional breweries and replaced them by national ones. In response to their own demands rather than those of the customers they reduced choice still further by cutting down the number of beers brewed. Small breweries today mostly produce more kinds of beer than big ones do.

Ten years ago there were 3,000 different beers on sale in Britain. There are now said to be 1,500 (the real choice is smaller because many are almost indistinguishable). It is true that because of reciprocal trading agreements between brewers an individual pub may now have a wider selection than previously, but in a given area the choice of traditional

draught beer available has inevitably declined with the
closure of local breweries. This does not only happen in
lightly-populated rural areas. As the 1969 Monopolies
Commission Report points out:

> Apart from small villages where the single public house
> has a local monopoly, there are a very few larger areas
> where the great majority of the public houses are owned
> by only one or two brewers. In the County Borough
> of Bristol, out of a total of 517 public houses, 461 are
> owned by brewers and over 90 per cent of these are
> owned by Courage, and Courage is the major supplier
> of beer to the free trade in that area also. In the County
> Borough of Birmingham, 729 of the 815 public houses
> are owned by the two brewers Bass (with 422 houses)
> and Allied (with 307 houses) and these two brewers
> are also the major suppliers to the free trade, which
> includes some 400 registered clubs and 86 public houses.

There are several other areas that the Monopolies Commission could have pointed to – the large parts of East
Anglia where whether what you want is Watney's or not
it's about all you can get; the areas of Hertfordshire and
Buckinghamshire that have only Ind Coope houses; and
so on. The Brewers' Society argued to the Monopolies
Commission that 'if the public is demanding a wider choice
of beers than a particular public house is providing, then
unless that pub offers characteristics which the consumers
rate more highly than breadth of choice, the effect must
be that it will lose trade to other outlets'. This is the language
of someone who has lost touch with reality. If you live in
Norfolk and like traditional draught beer it is little comfort
to know that Adnams make magnificent beer in Southwold.
Unless you are going to drive great distances to do your
drinking (a dangerous thing to do) then in large areas you
have the choice of going to a Watney's pub or not going to
a pub at all. The particular pub can hardly lose trade to
other outlets if there are no other outlets in reach. Without

the tied house system, which effectively gives the brewers control of the retail outlets, it would never have been so easy for them to impose their new products on the consumer.

That the consumer's interests have been threatened by the concentration in the industry and by the tied house system was recognized by the conclusion of the Monopolies Commission Report:

> We conclude that the conditions which we have found to prevail operate and may be expected to operate against the public interest since the restrictions on competition involved in the tied house system operated by the brewer suppliers concerned are detrimental to efficiency in brewing, wholesaling and retailing, to the interests of independent suppliers (including potential new entrants), and to the interests of consumers.

Centralization meant that beer had to travel further to the point of consumption. It was therefore a matter of convenience to the brewers, rather than the demand of the customers, that we should drink kinds of beer that travel well. The only problem was to get people to drink it, and this was done by massive and (it must be said) clever and amusing advertising which made almost indistinguishable products into household names. More than £1 million was spent on advertising Double Diamond alone in 1974, and others did not lag far behind. This massive advertising and skilful promotion increased the sale of keg beer from 1 per cent of the market in 1959 to over 20 per cent. Incidentally, the brewers' profit margin on keg beer, which usually costs 2p or 3p a pint more than traditional cask bitter, is about 50 per cent higher. It was this, rather than public demand, that made keg beer an attractive product for the brewers.

The preceding account would doubtless be disputed by the big brewers. They would argue that they have merely responded to a spontaneous demand for keg beer from customers. Evidence for this is thin: if keg-lovers exist they have not been vocal. A rare champion was Mr W. C. Stevenson, licensee of the Laughing Cavalier Inn, Stalybridge, Cheshire, who wrote a letter to the *Guardian* in February 1975 in defence of keg and top-pressure beer. He argued quite reasonably that it has such advantages as being less liable to contamination, has no ullage or spillage, and can be served in brewery condition irrespective of weather or cellar conditions. Having knocked traditional beer, he turns to the praise of keg: 'I and our customers have now acquired the taste for the modern chilled and filtered beer with very little effort, and consider the advantages mentioned above have made that little effort worth while.' To say that you can get used to something with a little effort is hardly reaching the heights of enthusiasm. Admittedly all beer is an acquired taste. That is to say, many people find that only after drinking it three or four times do they begin positively to enjoy it. Positively enjoying something is very different from learning to tolerate it, as Mr Stevenson and his customers appear to have done. His purely negative defence of keg beer supports my claim that customers have had to adapt themselves to the product, as opposed to the product satisfying the demands of the customer.

This is confirmed by the comments of objective commentators on the industry who may be considered less *parti pris* than I am. Kenneth Gooding, the *Financial Times* correspondent on the brewing industry, concluded an article (24 April 1974) on lager with the words: 'This rapid reduction of brands and the enormous sums spent promoting keg and lager ensure that it is lager and keg that the vast majority of beer drinkers will in future be drinking.' John Mark, lecturer in economics, Queen Elizabeth College, London, writes in *Lloyds Bank Review*, April 1974:

More tied outlets and larger distribution areas intensified

the problems of transporting and keeping the beer: these were tackled mainly by infusing draught beer with carbon dioxide at the brewery and serving the beer under pressure (known as 'keg' beer). These keg beers keep longer and can be widely distributed. The extra outlets and larger areas also *required the customer to be persuaded* to accept national products, recognizably different from the traditional ales, and this factor increased the role of marketing and advertising. If demand could be increased for a single brew, yielding economies of scale in production, it simultaneously diminished the demand for local brews, whose producers could not afford comparable advertising expenditure. The financial power of the major companies, especially in marketing, is a crucial factor in recent years.

(My italics)

Such was the theory. Where did it go wrong?

First, it was found that economies of scale worked both ways. It is true that it requires no more labour to watch a large kettle boil than it does to watch a small one. It is equally true that a tiny dispute can bring a large brewery to a halt as easily as a small one. Perhaps more easily, for the big brewing companies have been bedevilled by industrial disputes in recent years, and with centralized production they have found themselves at the mercy of the draymen who distribute the beer to the pubs. Large areas of the country in recent years have repeatedly been deprived of beer supplies because of disputes between big brewing companies and their employees. On the other hand the small breweries appear to have unusually good labour relations. I have made enquiries at several small breweries about industrial disputes and repeatedly received the same answer: 'Never have any'.

Professor Vaizey, by getting it all wrong, makes the point nicely. In the old-established family firms, he says,

Traditional patterns and loyalties limit the seizing of

profit opportunities . . . The influence of the family is usually twofold. First, they are representatives of the original firm; because members of these families, educated at the older Universities or at Sandhurst, are still on the Board, there are some restraints against commercial pushfulness, and an emphasis on dealing 'properly' with employees and the public.

The idea of behaving 'properly' to employees and the public must have seemed very alien to go-ahead brewers and economists in the late 1950s, but it is one that some of these family firms still cling to. In some cases they may be accused of being paternalistic, sometimes even downright reactionary. They are rarely enamoured of trade unions. In one such firm, where all the directors have the same surname, they are addressed as Mr Michael, Mr Robert, Mr Peter and so on. The Head Brewer, who has been working there for nearly half a century, is addressed as Mr Jenkins. This may seem comically nineteenth-century, but big brewers, economists or anyone else inclined to laugh at such antiquated relationships might find it salutory to look at this firm's record of industrial disputes – virtually none.

A big modern brewery employs very few people in a very large area. Going round them always gives you the impression that it must be the lunch hour: there's nobody about. There are few workers and they usually do one specialized task, probably watching dials. The vacuum created by removing individual skill is filled by boredom. By contrast, a small brewery offers varied and skilled work in a pleasant atmosphere with plenty of human contact. Small breweries give the impression that they are places where it would be fun to work. When the job of head brewer is advertised for one of them there are usually several applications from employees of big breweries who are prepared to take considerable drops in salary to work in more pleasant surroundings and produce better beer.

George Bateman's is a family brewery in Lincolnshire with 140 pubs. At the time of the firm's centenary in 1974 no fewer than twelve members of its work-force of 98 had more than 25 years' service with the firm; two brothers had a combined service of 82 years, another three employees had been there 50 years, and the secretary and director for 38 years. They brew first-rate beer, too.

Young's of Wandsworth is another such family firm. One of its employees represents the eighth generation of his family to work there, and the Young family has been running the brewery for about as long. One old chap is still working there at the age of 80: he has retired three times but keeps coming back because he enjoys the work, is good at it, and the firm is humane and flexible enough not to refuse to employ someone simply because of his chronological age.

The traditional techniques of this brewery make the work more varied, more skilled and more satisfying than those of a big modern beer-factory. The enthusiastic and affable personality of the chairman, John Young, is to be felt everywhere. Like any efficient business, this one is geared to making money, but it is not *just* geared to making money. It has much that might not impress cost-accountants. The Ram Brewery has 80 Muscovy ducks, several guinea-fowl, two geese called Engelbert and Humperdinck, a few cats, a goat, a fine ram called Ram Rod (the brewery mascot and symbol) and 27 magnificent shire horses. As for cost-accountants, a work study has shown that within a few miles of a brewery the horse-drawn drays are more economical than motor transport.

One doesn't want to give the impression that Young's brewery is all farmyard animals. Like any other it also has big machines, and they are as beautiful as any I've seen. The 1835 beam engine, its copper and brass gleaming like coronation regalia, is thought to be the oldest working steam engine in the country, and is still running as efficiently as ever on its wooden cogs (hornbeam). The larger engine, known as 'the new engine', dates from 1867.

If this is not the kind of thing that impresses those of Professor Vaizey's way of thinking, they might consider the fact that sales of Young's beer increased by some 20 per cent in 1974–5 as against a national average of ·89 per cent. It is breweries of just this kind of size that the Big Six have closed down as uneconomic.

George II said to someone who complained that General Wolfe was mad, 'Oh! he is mad, is he? Then I wish he would bite some other of my generals.' There must be many shareholders and directors of the Big Six breweries who wish they could produce beer as uneconomically as the small ones do.

Small units are more efficient in all kinds of ways. A Yorkshire publican was complaining recently that 'When companies were smaller we could take our business to the top man. Now you have to give three months' notice to see a lad at the bottom.' (*Morning Advertiser*, 10 October 1975). It makes a great difference both to employees and customers to know that the boss is there every day. In some cases he actually does the brewing, like Christopher Hyde of Hydes' Anvil Brewery, Manchester, or Claude Arkell of the Donnington Brewery, who also delivers the beer by van in person when necessary. It is not at all the same to know that the boss is sipping claret over lunch in a boardroom at the top of a skyscraper in London. The short chain of command means that the small brewery is more flexible and responsive to the customers' demands and that it is truly operating in the classic market conditions of supply and demand. If Bill in the Public Bar of The Swan at Much Toping says his pint is off, the guv'nor has only to pick up the phone and the Head Brewer will know in ten minutes. He might well decide to drop in at lunchtime and taste it himself. It's very different from the world of Maxwell Joseph.

Department of Employment statistics show that the annual average for days lost from industrial disputes in manufacturing industry in 1971-3 increased from 15 days per 1,000 employees in plants employing 10-25 workers, to more than 2,000 days in plants employing 1,000 or more. There are many other ways in which small units are preferable to big ones, and they are not recent discoveries. Gandhi was saying these things a long time ago. Only late in the 1960s, however, did it become respectable to question the worship of bigness. An article by Peter Marr and Stephen Fineman of the MRC Social and Applied Psychology Unit at the University of Sheffield showed a change in the conventional academic wisdom. Called 'Mergers: why the bigger isn't the better' (*Marketing*, November 1970) it includes some obvious discoveries, some less so.

Organizations are made up of human beings, and human beings do not work according to simple economic rules. They are moved by quite different forces which often operate against the economic and financial principles which management pundits hold so dear . . . Recent United States figures reveal that big business has now fallen behind small business in terms of the return which is provided on stockholder's equity . . . There is now evidence from several studies of a strong inverse relationship between company size and return on assets . . . Arguments about the 'economies of scale' and about 'industrial logic' may have some virtue, but they are not laws of nature . . . There is no doubt that arguments which are rational in an economic sense are rarely the basic motivation for mergers. Underlying the surface reasons there is generally a set of personal desires for acquisition, power, self-advancement and visible signs of social progress . . . People in very large units are socially and mentally *less* well-off than their counterparts . . . Very large units are slow and ponderous

. . . [The individual] is likely to feel alienated and frustrated in the very large unit.

Much of this analysis has been confirmed by the comparative fortunes of large and small breweries in the past five years. The small firms have suffered from the disadvantages of higher prices for raw materials and cash-flow problems holding up new developments. On the other hand they are able to provide their customers in the free and tied trade with a more flexible and more personal service; they have lower transport costs and far fewer industrial disputes; and they produce a kind of beer that increasing numbers of customers are prepared if necessary to seek out. The big brewers have found that the advantages of size are limited; one economist has calculated that a brewery producing 3 per cent of the total output of the industry has achieved maximum efficiency in terms of taking advantage of large-scale production. There are no advantages in being bigger than that. At the same time these centralized breweries now have the problem of transport, the cost of which has gone up for the first time since the Middle Ages. The effect of all this will take time to show, but it is obvious that in the coming years it will make less sense rather than more to have enormous breweries in the middle of England and to carry very large quantities of water (which is what beer mostly consists of) about the country in vehicles running on expensive and irreplaceable fossil fuels.

The small breweries that really were inefficient fell by the wayside long ago. The survivors are tough and, while they and their customers remain confident in their product, their scale and their traditional product give them positive advantages over the bigger firms. This is one of the surprises that the big brewers have received in the last two or three years. The other is that significant numbers of supposedly malleable consumers have revolted and made their preference for real beer apparent enough to be perceived even by accountants and economists.

Traditional draught beer has become something of a craze, especially among students and unmarried men in their twenties. To some extent it may therefore be a transitory phenomenon. What CND was in the early 1960s, Camra has been in the mid-1970s. Perhaps in ten years' time Camra will have dwindled to as minuscule a body as CND is today. However, one should remember that CND's decline can in part be explained by the fact that it largely achieved its objectives. It is true that Britain did not unilaterally give up nuclear weapons, that we are still under the threat of nuclear annihilation, and that the Test Ban Treaty was not the work of CND. On the other hand, CND and the Committee of 100 did manage to alert the consciousness of a previously ignorant and apathetic public to the very present danger to themselves and the future health of their children. CND could not prevent the Cuba crisis, but it did make sure that every nursing mother knew what Strontium 90 was. On a different plane, Camra couldn't stop the Barnsley Brewery being closed down, but at least every self-respecting beer-drinker now knows the difference between keg and traditional cask beer.

I said earlier that most of the complaints in the 1960s were about what the brewers were doing to pubs rather than to the beer. There were some protests, however, from the moment the brewers started gassing everything in sight, and credit should be given to the alert and discerning pubmen who made their lonely voices heard in those early days. As long ago as 1963 a letter in the *Financial Times* complained about the use of extraneous CO_2 in the serving of draught beer, and the same year saw the formation of a group called the Society for the Preservation of Beer from the Wood (SPBW – sometimes affectionately known as SPQR).

Though well-intentioned, the initial aims of the SPBW were a little misguided. Wooden casks are picturesque, and give better temperature insulation than metal ones. Otherwise they are rather a nuisance to all concerned: to the publican because they are so heavy, and to the brewer because they are hard to sterilize and therefore more liable to infection. In due course the SPBW transferred its efforts to attacking extraneous CO_2 rather than defending wood, but they were stuck with a name that gave the impression that they were barking up the wrong tree. Nevertheless, by its very existence the SPBW demonstrated that there was an opposition to what the brewers were doing. In the autumn of 1972 the brewers obligingly brought this opposition to the attention of the general public. The SPBW tried to take a stall at a commercially-organized beer exhibition at the Alexandra Palace, but were excluded because of the objections of brewers who were exhibiting fizzy beer. The SPBW were joined by the newly-formed Campaign for the Revitalization of Ale (as Camra was then called) in picketing the Ally Pally. The two organizations won far more publicity by being kept out than if they had been let in.

Also at the end of the 1960s some of the independent breweries – Adnams of Southwold, Greene King of Bury St Edmunds, Boddingtons' in Manchester, Young's in Wandsworth and a handful of others – took the quite deliberate decision to stick to the traditional products they were proud of rather than, as some of the small breweries did, go a-whoring after the monopolists. In his annual report to the shareholders of Greene King in 1971 the managing director said: '. . . our real draught beer is growing in popularity in competition with the so-called premium keg beers of some of our competitors. As most drinkers know, traditional draught beer has more character and flavour than filtered and pasteurized keg beer and is generally cheaper too.'

Not to be forgotten in any pre-history of the campaign for real beer is Becky's Dive Bar, named after its delightful

proprietress Mrs Rebecca Willeter. This decrepit free house
was at 24 Southwark Street SE1 in the basement of the Hop
Exchange. To reach it you had to go down a dingy staircase
which ended in several collapsed steps. Unfavourable
first impressions were soon revised. It was crowded, but
with discerning people. There was music, but not the slushy
muzak or zillion-decibel juke-box that has ruined so many
establishments. Instead a gramophone was playing one of
Becky's large collection of records, many of them 78s.
George Formby was cleaning windows, followed by 'Run,
Rabbit, Run' and then the incomparable Fats Waller.
In the evenings there was often live music and singing.

The decor was not exactly David Hicks, but that's not
a bad thing. Like the gramophone records, it had a 1940s'
atmosphere suggestive of air-raid sirens and blackouts. If a
gas-mask had been hanging on the wall it would not have
looked out of place. In the lounge bar there was a piano
and a three-piece suite of big brown leather armchairs and
sofa with broken springs. If someone had wanted to film
a scene of the British people at home listening phleg-
matically to Churchill's wartime speeches on a cathedral-
like wireless, this would have been the place. All you would
have needed to do was to shift the barrels, which were
everywhere. For what made the Dive Bar unique was not
the decor or the music but the beer. Becky claimed to have
250 different kinds to choose from – beer from all over
Europe ('I've been in the Common Market for a long
time,' she said); beer from Singapore, Czechoslovakia,
Australia and Poland; Kronenbourg from France, San
Miguel from Spain and even Dublin-bottled Guinness.
'You can go for a pub-crawl in my pub,' Becky would say.

As well as all these bottled beers she had draught bitter
from three brewers which at that time supplied no one
else in central London – Shepherd Neame of Faversham,
Thwaites of Blackburn and Ruddle's of Rutland. Later
others were added. They were put up on the counter,

and the beer was served directly from the casks by gravity.

The Hop Exchange itself is an imposing building dating from 1866 and since the demolition of the Coal Exchange in 1963 the only one of its kind left in London. The owners, Joe Lyons, have long had plans to restore its pristine glory. Unfortunately these plans threatened the Dive, and an uncertain future meant that it became ever more dilapidated. There were complaints about hygiene, and the Gents was past a joke. This did not prevent a Becky's cult developing, and the Dive received a further boost on becoming a finalist in the 1974 *Evening Standard* Pub of the Year competition. Success had the unusual, and characteristic, effect of making the place even dingier than before. In the summer of 1975 it closed down. I trust that by the time this book is published the Dive will have had a Phoenix-like rebirth.

There were some who loathed the Dive, and far more who loved it. Whatever else you might say against it, this was one place that was not Laodicean. It had guts, character, friendliness and conviviality, all emanating from the personalities of Becky herself and her robust and genial barman Harry. In addition to creating a great pub out of the sandwich bar Becky took over in 1954, they made it a living gallery of beer from all over England, more than ten years before anyone else did anything similar. Thereby the Dive performed a great educational service.

By 1972 criticism of the big brewers in the form of news reports and letters in the national, regional and local press was becoming increasingly frequent. The more paranoid members of the Brewers' Society (and that's *very* paranoid) claimed it was all a concerted conspiracy by a tightly-knit body. One of them was apparently convinced that the whole thing was financed by the chairman of one of the independent breweries (I won't embarrass him by naming him). Nothing could be further from the truth. What happened was that a number of very different people who had no connection with one another woke up to the same conclusions at roughly the same time. When I started my beer column in the *Guardian* in August 1973 I had never heard of Christopher Hutt, whose admirably angry book *The Death of the English Pub* appeared not long afterwards. No more had I heard of Frank Baillie, whose factual *Beer Drinker's Companion* provided an essential guide to those roaming the country in search of good beer. I had heard of Camra and the SPBW but beyond the mere fact of their existence I knew nothing else about them.

Similarly Camra was originally set up in ignorance of the existence of the SPBW. It was formed rather half-heartedly in 1971 by four young northerners under the name of the Campaign for the Revitalization of Ale. Their original intention was the extremely odd one of saving the word 'ale' which for reasons I do not understand they preferred to the word 'beer', perhaps under the erroneous impression that beer is a southern word and therefore effete.

Later it occurred to them that if they were going to save the word they had better try and save the thing itself. They soon showed a considerable flair for publicity and membership rose from some 200 in 1972 to 2,300 in July 1973.

At first the brewers replied to criticisms in the press with petulant rebuttals, but after being worsted in the letters columns of various newspapers (especially the *Guardian* and the *Financial Times*), they retired from that knockabout arena with bloody noses and, as far as public utterances were concerned, retreated into sullen silence. In private, they howled with rage. Recently a spokesman for the industry said that he had always welcomed the interest shown by Camra in the cause of good beer. This was about as convincing as if ex-President Thieu issued a statement welcoming the Viet Cong's interest in the politics of South Vietnam. Though sweetness and light now prevail, three years ago I met with nothing but hostility from the big brewers (with the honourable exception of Guinness), and I know that Camra had the same experience.

That more than a very small bunch of people were involved became apparent to me personally within a few weeks of starting my column. A deluge of letters from readers made it apparent beyond conceivable doubt that whether or not I was doing the job well, it was a job that many people wanted to be done. It was clear too that, contrary to the statements of the Brewers' Society and the press officers of the big companies, there was a vast number of people who had found themselves deprived of the kind of beer they prefer. This was also reflected in the rapid growth of Camra's membership – from 2,300 members in July 1973 to 18,000 a year later and 30,000 by the end of the year, at around which figure it seems to have levelled off. (Enquiries about membership should be addressed to CAMRA, 34 Alma Road, St Albans, Herts).

Camra has sometimes taken itself too seriously, and too solemnly. It has often been too doctrinaire, and at times shown signs of confusing beer with religion (one of its leading members used to speak of 'spreading the gospel of Camra'). Some individual members have emerged as bores of Olympic standard. In fairness, Camra has usually been quick to face up to its own faults and do something about them. Generally its record has been one of extraordinary success. It now has a full-time staff of some ten people, and more than 100 branches throughout the country. Its monthly newspaper is energetically edited by Michael Hardman, one of Camra's founding members. Camra has launched a property company which now owns and runs several pubs of its own. It has published national and local guides to pubs with real beer, and organized several extremely successful beer festivals. Most important of all, it has become an effective pressure group spearheading a consumer revolt which extends far beyond its membership. Michael Young, chairman of the National Consumer

Council, has been quoted as saying that Camra is 'the most successful consumer organization in Western Europe.'

It is hard to assess the exact impact of this unique consumer revolt. In terms of pints sold the real beer revival has been far less significant than the rapid increase in sales of lager, which has gone up from virtually nothing in the early 1960s to somewhere around 18 per cent in 1975: predictions are that by the end of the decade one pint in in four will be lager. But the rise of lager was predicted, planned for and vigorously promoted, whereas the revival of traditional cask-conditioned draught beer was totally unexpected by all but a very few, and some brewers positively resisted it. Indeed, for some time the brewing industry as a whole made strenuous attempts to deny that any such thing was happening. Those who claimed that the consumers' interests were suffering were subjected to abuse and hostility from the big-wigs of the industry, which was naturally reciprocated. They attributed all sorts of motives except the real one, a concern about deterioration in the national beverage.

The big brewing companies (and, it should not be forgotten, some of the small ones) preferred to listen to their accountants and marketing men, who told them what they wanted to hear. Their behaviour uniquely combined that of an ostrich with King Canute's. Finally (if I can maintain this confused metaphor) their heads were removed from the sand by the incoming waves. Now they are all trying to jump on the bandwagon – or the horse-drawn brewer's dray. Real beer is busting out all over. Three years ago it was big news for beer freaks when the landlord of a free house put back the hand pumps. Now such an event is so frequent as to go unremarked, except of course by the customers who invariably increase in number as a result. The news nowadays is rather that the demand for hand pumps is so great that there is a shortage. Two years ago small companies producing traditional beer were often rather ashamed of still doing so; now they vaunt the fact. Those that thought they were keeping abreast of the times by abandoning real beer (going 'all bright' was the phrase) have had to go into reverse. Everards of Leicester, for example, ceased to brew traditional cask beer altogether: in the summer of 1975 they reverted to it with a powerful draught bitter called Old Original. Two years ago Paine and Co. of St Neots was selling its beer under top-pressure in all but one of its tied houses: since then they have changed back to means of dispense that do not involve extraneous CO_2. Several small breweries have introduced new traditionally-brewed beers. The independent brewers of real beer have reported enormous increases in sales, and have turned in equally satisfactory financial reports. Several companies that a few years ago were totally demoralized and resigned to being taken over and closed down by one of the Big Six, have now discovered a new excitement, pride and confidence. The credit for this is due almost entirely to the consumer revolt.

Nor have the monolithic Big Six been unaffected. Courage's have presented the remarkable spectacle of replacing hand pumps in pubs from which only recently they were tearing them out. Their excellent Director's bitter had become almost impossible to find, and even then was full of bubbles. The brewery certainly did not promote it and several publicans have told me that they were actively discouraged from keeping it. I am satisfied in my own mind that Courage's at one point were intent on phasing out Director's altogether. Then early in 1975 came a sudden switch in policy. Hand-pumped Director's was introduced to 30 London pubs and hand-pumped Best Bitter to 30 pubs in the Reading area. This was done as an experiment, and at the time of its launching a director of Courage's told me it would give customers an opportunity to express their preference: this implied that the opportunity did not exist before, something he had always hotly denied.

The other five big companies have each responded in their own way to the demand for real beer. The most extraordinary case is that of Watney's. Having entirely eliminated real beer from their pubs in large areas of the country they cast themselves in the role of chief villains, and the name of Watney's became synonymous with everything unpleasant in the brewing industry. Mr Maxwell Joseph of Grand Metropolitan Hotels, which owns Watney's, complained of a word-of-mouth campaign against the brewery. One could retort that it is more a matter of taste-in-the-mouth. For many years Watney's spent enormous sums of money on associating their name with the colour red: the pubs were all painted red, the beer was called Watney's Red and so on. Early in 1975 many of their pubs in London were repainted in any colour other than red. The company appeared to be trying to camouflage its pubs, to conceal the fact that they were Watney's houses. I can think of no parallel for such behaviour in any industry. Meanwhile in the North of England, where some years ago Wilson's pubs were turned into Watney's, they are now being switched back into Wilson's again. The name of Watney's must have acquired exceptionally bad vibrations to make this necessary. More positively, the company has been trying out real beer in parts of the country where they had previously eliminated it, to see if there is a demand. It seems that they have discovered that there is. As Lichtenburg puts it in one of his aphorisms, there are some people who won't listen until their ears are cut off.

Another encouraging sign is the fact that for the first time for many years new breweries are being started up. A couple of years ago there were only four pubs in the country that brewed their own beer: these were the All Nations Inn, Madeley, Telford, Shropshire; the Blue Anchor Inn, Helston, Cornwall; the Old Swan, Netherton, Dudley; and the Three Tuns, Bishop's Castle, Shropshire. In the summer of 1975 the Mason Arms in South Liegh,

Witney, Oxfordshire started brewing its own beer. Later
in the year brewing began at the Fighting Cocks, Corby
Glen, near Grantham, Lincolnshire. This pub belongs
to a company called Brewpubs Ltd, formed by Roger
Booth, who brewed for some years for Nimmo's in
Durham, and later started the Tom Caxton home-brew kit.

In 1976 brewing began at the Miskin Arms, Miskin,
Pontyclun, Glamorgan, and at the New Fermor Arms,
Rufford, near Ormskirk, Lancashire.

The Miners' Arms at Priddy in Somerset is slightly
different because it is a restaurant rather than a pub. It's
hard to find but worth the effort. Telephone Priddy 217,
not just to book a table but for instructions on how to
find the place. As well as Paul Leyton's own beer you can
eat snails collected, prepared and cooked by him, home-
cured ham and other local produce. The brewery, which
is tiny and rather Heath Robinsonish, produces a mere
five gallons or so a week, but Mr Leyton deserves credit as
a pioneer, since he took out his licence to brew as long ago
as 1973.

The Litchborough Brewing Company was started in
1974 in Northamptonshire by Bill Urquhart, who was made
redundant after 40 years in brewing when Watney's
closed down its Northampton brewery. Recently, David
Pollard has started brewing commercially in Reddish, near
Stockport, and John Boothroyd's beer and wine-makers'
shop in York is brewing a high-gravity, naturally conditioned bottled beer called York Brewery Extra Strong
Traditional Real Ale. More small breweries and home-brew
pubs can be expected before long.

Only three years ago the prospect was extremely grim.
The fear that we would soon all be drinking the same
Eurofizz beer, from the west coast of Ireland to the Urals,
was perhaps exaggerated, but it did look as though real
beer was going to become as hard to find as real bread,
real cheese, and other victims of the mid-twentieth century.

Suddenly and astonishingly it made a comeback. Hand-pumped beer has been installed in two London railway stations. They have even put in hand pumps at the Bull in Ambridge.

The success of the consumer revolt is important not just to beer drinkers but to everybody who is concerned about the quality of life. If it can be done with beer it can be done with other things. We do not have to behave as accountants and economists think we ought to behave. You *can* stand in the way of progress.

V Beer in the Home

Though the natural habitat of beer is the pub, it also thrives in captivity. For most people this simply means keeping a few tins of lager in the fridge for use in summer, but if you want to be more ambitious it is easy to build up an interesting beer cellar. There is no point in laying down ordinary carbonated bottled beer since, far from maturing, it will begin to deteriorate after a few weeks. There are a few beers you can lay down for years to come, such as the strong living beers already mentioned – Courage's Russian Imperial Stout, Eldridge Pope's Thomas Hardy Ale and Gale's Prize Old Ale.

For general consumption it will be useful to have half a dozen bottles of Guinness and half a dozen White Shield Worthington, which are both sediment beers, and some Newcastle Brown. As you travel about the country it is always worth buying a few bottles of the strong beers and barley wines of the small independent breweries for drinking on cold evenings.

If you live within easy distance of a pub that sells good beer, then why not take a jug along and get some draught beer for your Sunday lunch? A half-gallon wine jar is ideal; the landlord will appreciate it if you take a funnel along to help him fill it, and also if you don't ask him at the very busiest moment of the week. Real draught beer will keep perfectly well for several days. If you're having a party, or just have a few thirsty people about, then it's worth getting a cask of real beer from your friendly publican or local brewery. A pin (36 pints) will keep quite satisfactorily for a week to ten days, but it requires a certain amount of skill in tapping and spiling, and needs a day or two to settle before you start drinking it.

What may be more convenient is a polypin, 36 pints of real beer in a plastic container which collapses about the beer as it is drawn off. This means that there is no need for an air-hole and that the beer therefore never comes into contact with the atmosphere. It should keep for up to three weeks without trouble. Brewers producing polypins of real beer include Young's, Shepherd Neame, King and Barnes, Fuller, Smith and Turner and Harveys.

I'm not usually very fond of tinned beer, but this is because of the beer rather than the container. The big brewers' tinned beers that advertising has made into household names are sweet, fizzy, and usually taste more of caramel and cardboard than malt and hops. Some of the independent brewers produce bottled and tinned beer that are far more like the real thing. Particularly commendable is the Marks and Spencer's range which has low carbonation and is brewed without the use of any adjuncts. The packaging is unusually attractive and declares the original gravity and alcoholic contents. The Lancashire Light Ale is light in colour, not gassy, and with a very clean taste: it is brewed by Thwaites of Blackburn. The Export Pale Ale and Yorkshire Strong Ale are brewed by Sam Smith's, Tadcaster. The Suffolk Strong Pale Ale is brewed by Greene King, and the Special Country Bitter and Rutland Brown Ale are the work of Ruddle's.

1   Brew It Yourself

When William Cobbett wrote *Cottage Economy* in 1821 his aim was to improve the lot of the rural labourer by giving simple instructions in what used to be called do-it-yourself and is now known more portentously as self-sufficiency. There are many such books nowadays; Cobbett's is not only one of the first but still one of the best. He covers everything from how to make bread and candles to how to keep cows and pigs, turkeys, pigeons, goats and ewes. The first, and longest, section of the book is on brewing. 'In former times,' Cobbett writes,

> to set about to show to Englishmen that it was good for them to brew beer in their homes would have been as impertinent as gravely to insist that they ought to endeavour not to lose their breath; for in those times (only forty years ago) to have a house and not to brew was a rare thing indeed.

> Mr Ellman, an old man and a large farmer in Sussex, has recently given in Evidence before a Committee of the House of Commons this fact, that forty years ago, there was not a labourer in his parish that did not brew his own beer; and that now, there is not one that does it, except by chance the malt be given him. The cause of this change has been the lowering of the wages of labour, compared with the price of provisions, by the means of the paper money, the enormous tax upon the barley when made into malt, and the increased tax upon hops. These have quite changed the custom of the English people as to their drink. They still drink beer, but, in general, it is of the brewing of common brewers ...

Home brewing had declined with the growth of the commercial brewers in the eighteenth century. Cobbett set out to revive it. He contrasts the manliness of beer-drinking with the 'pernicious practice of drinking tea'. The beer drinker will be cheaply and well nourished, and will also have such useful by-products as yeast for baking and spent grains for his pigs. Tea, on the other hand, is not only without nutritional value, but also causes sleeplessness, weakens the nerves, and is expensive – which indeed it was, at five shillings a pound. Cobbett backs up his assertions by suggesting that you try out an experiment on a pig. If you feed it on the malt from which a year's supply of beer is made 'he will repay you in ten score of bacon or there-abouts'. If, on the other hand, you tried feeding him on a year's supply of tea, then 'he is dead with hunger, and bequeaths you his skeleton at the end of about seven days'.

Tea causes sleeplessness and weakens the nerves. It demands constant fire-making, which is expensive and time-consuming. Cobbett estimates that the tea-drinker must make 200 fires a year that he would not otherwise have made:

It is impossible to make a fire, boil water, make the tea, drink it, wash up the things, sweep up the fireplace and put all to rights again in a less space of time, upon an average, than two hours. However, let us allow one hour: and here we have a woman occupied no less than three hundred and sixty-five hours in the year, or thirty whole days, at twelve hours in the day, besides the waste in the man's time in hanging about waiting for the tea!

He produces similar computations to demonstrate the economic advantages of home brewing, the product of which is not only more beneficial than tea but also 'as strong as the generality of the beer to be had at the public house, and divested of the poisonous drugs which that beer too often contains', having been concocted by 'beer-doctors' and 'brewers' druggists'.

Even when Cobbett was writing, about half the beer in the country was still brewed at home, but in spite of his efforts home-brewing continued to decline and the commercial brewers to grow. Finally came Gladstone's Inland Revenue Act of 1880, which entangled the home brewer in such a tiresome web of petty restrictions, taxes and licences that, combined with the shortages of two world wars, by the middle of this century home brewing was virtually extinct.

Virtually, but not quite. It continued clandestinely, and

probably on a much wider scale than is generally thought. Why else did chemists sell so much malt extract in the post-war years? And why did so many people buy plain malt in preference to the kind with cod liver oil in it, which was beneficial in medical terms but not brewing ones?

Then came April 1963, a date revered by home brewers. It was in the Budget of that month and year that Mr Reginald Maudling took the opportunity of being Chancellor of the Exchequer to set the home brewer free. Henceforward anyone could brew as much beer, and beer as strong, as he liked. The only restriction was on its sale.

Since that memorable day home brewing has developed enormously. Twenty million gallons (160 million pints) of beer were brewed in the home in 1973, and by now it has probably topped the 200 million pints. This is about 1 or 2 per cent of the beer brewed in the country, the equivalent to the year's production of a medium-sized brewery. About three-quarters of it is made from kits, most of which are sold by Boots.

The reasons for brewing your own beer are the same as those for baking your own bread, growing your own vegetables, making your own clothes or doing your own carpentry. Because these are creative activities, they are fun. They also save money: home-brewed beer costs about a quarter of the price of commercial beer, and even less if you buy in bulk. Since commercial beer is taxed according to strength, and the home brewer can make his beer stronger merely by adding sugar, in terms of alcohol for money the difference is even greater. After a small initial outlay for equipment you should be able to brew five gallons of strong beer for about £1·60 – say, 4p a pint.

Of course a low price is no consolation if the stuff is undrinkable, and there is no denying that the home brewer is capable of producing liquids of unspeakable foulness. Even the very best home brew will not be as good as the very best products of the professional brewer, simply

because the professionals have more skill and better
equipment, and there are problems about brewing on a
small scale: there is indeed an identifiable 'small-scale
flavour.' Having said that, one must add that the best
home brews are very good indeed, and that even the run-
of-the-mill home brew made from a kit has real advantages
over most commercial bottled beers, since it is a traditionally-brewed living beer. In unfortunate parts of the
country where a virtual monopoly is maintained by one
national brewer who sells no real beer, home brewing may
become a matter not of choice but necessity.

Cobbett recommended the home brewer to invest in a
rather complicated brewing-machine. He goes into great
detail about the machine's workings and extols it so effu-
sively that he feels impelled to explain that he has no
financial interest in the thing: 'In pointing out the many and
great advantages of the Machine, I have solely the public
good in view.' Having finished with the subject of brewing
he goes on to a host of subjects from the keeping of cows to
the keeping of bees. Finally, at the very end of the book (it
originally appeared in monthly parts) he returns in a brief
paragraph to the subject of brewing:

> N.B. Having, in the former Numbers, spoken of brewing-
> machines, I cannot conclude my Work without stating,
> that further experience has induced me to resolve to
> discontinue the use of all sorts of brewing-machines,
> and to use the old sort of utensils.

Today there is even less need to be deterred by the need
for special equipment. For the complete beginner it is
probably as well to start with a kit, easily available from
home-brewing shops, many supermarkets and most branches
of Boots. In addition to the kit you'll need some sugar, a
clean (preferably new) five-gallon plastic dustbin, ordinary
kitchen equipment and the ability to follow simple instructions on the back of a packet.

The first operation consists of boiling up the malt and

hops. This will fill the house with a delicious aroma. If your spouse dislikes it, change your spouse. After a given time (about 30–45 minutes) strain the liquid into a clean plastic dustbin which has been sterilized with Campden tablets. Add the sugar, top up with cold water, add brewer's yeast, cover and leave in a warm place (about 60–65 degrees Fahrenheit). This operation will have taken at most an hour, during most of which all you have to do is watch the cauldron boiling.

For the next five days or so the brew goes through a violent yeasty ferment. Finally its rage subsides and, as in Beethoven's *Pastoral Symphony*, a peaceful calm ensues. The process of clarifying will have been helped by adding a small quantity of isinglass. When fermentation is complete, the beer is syphoned into clean bottles to which you add sugar (about half a teaspoon to the pint) to cause a secondary fermentation. There are cheap plastic caps that seal bottles satisfactorily. For a more professional look, you can invest in a crown capping machine. I do not recommend the kind that involves the use of a hammer: the inevitable broken bottles are at best messy and at worst dangerous. Screw-topped beer or cider flagons are ideal but hard to come by nowadays. If you are taking the thing seriously you can splash out a fiver or so on a special home brewer's semi-transparent plastic barrel. These save a great deal of time, and bottling is the most time-consuming and tedious process in home-brewing. What above all you must not do is to use a spirits bottle or any other kind that is not designed to withstand pressure: if you do, you run the risk of the bottle exploding, which is wasteful, messy and dangerous.

After about ten days, the bottled beers will have settled and should be quite clear and ready for drinking; the larger quantity in a barrel may take longer to clear. Open the bottle, pour carefully and steadily so as not to disturb the sediment. Drink. Repeat until satisfied.

Some people find kits perfectly satisfactory and go on using them for brew after brew. The more adventurous will want to branch out on their own. It is cheaper to buy the ingredients individually and in bigger quantities, and by buying the precise quality of malt and hops you like you can make beer that is suited exactly to your own taste. A very simple recipe that I have used several times with success consists of 6oz of hops, 5lb of dry malt extract and yeast. Because of the large quantity of malt, no sugar is needed. The really skilled home brewer who is prepared to go to the trouble can produce a beer of exactly the appearance, flavour and strength he likes – not just once, but over and over again. The best home brews are not made from malt extract but, as the professionals do, from malt. This involves mashing, which needs special equipment, and a little more time and trouble. The finer details of home brewing are fully explained in the several good books on the subject that are currently available.

In conclusion, a brief word about strength. Beginners often get carried away by the ease with which you can produce strong beer. All you have to do is add more sugar. There are two disadvantages, though. One is that too much sugar impairs the flavour. The other is that for normal purposes beer is a long drink, and you don't want something that will put you to sleep after two pints. It should take at least four.

2 The Cook's Ale

Since the Second World War English cooking has been greatly improved by recipes and ingredients from abroad. Foreign holidays and proliferating French, Italian, Spanish, Indian and Chinese restaurants have introduced us (or in some cases reintroduced us) to all kinds of new flavours. The enormously educational work of Elizabeth David and subsequent cookery writers has made olive oil and garlic into things for which the people who begin at Calais are no longer despised but positively envied, and the housewife with a bottle of wine on the kitchen shelf is now more likely to be taken for a competent cook than an incipient alcoholic. How far these changes go beyond the kitchens of the middle class is doubtful, but it is still true that our first steps into Europe were made gastronomically well before they were economically, and in the kitchen at least the consequences have been unarguably beneficial.

At times, however, it has seemed that while embracing foreign ways we have been in danger of forgetting our native traditions. The trendies of the swinging sixties could be relied on to turn out a passable *coq au vin*, but did they know how to cook a steak-and-kidney pudding? Fortunately in the last few years cookery writers have begun to give proper attention to English cookery. Almost without exception, however, while recommending English ingredients and English recipes they ignore English drinks. If they tell you to use alcohol in a dish it is (with the exception of cider with ham) almost invariably wine, which seems to me somehow inappropriate for Lancashire hot-pot, say, or shepherd's pie, or steak-and-kidney pudding.

Doubtless this results in part from force of habit: now that the wine-bottle has won its rightful place in the kitchen its use has become fairly automatic. Another reason may be that most cookery writers – certainly most of the best cookery writers – are women, and for the last 100 years women have usually been conditioned not to like beer – just as men are conversely conditioned to associate it with manliness. This is a pity, and rather silly. What I try to do here is simply to suggest that beer belongs on the kitchen shelf every bit as much as wine does. It is a delicious ingredient in many dishes, and incidentally it is considerably cheaper to splash beer around than even the most ordinary of cooking wines.

The reasons for using beer in cooking are the same as

marjoram, knotted-marjoram, and a leaf or two of sage), some onions, cloves, and Cayenne; cover it close, and simmer till quite tender: two or three hours will do it. When done lay it into a deep dish, set it over hot water, and cover it close. Skim the gravy; put in a few pickled mushrooms, truffles, morels, and oysters, if agreeable, but it is very good without; thicken the gravy with flour and butter, and heat it with the above, and pour over the beef. Forcemeat-balls of veal, anchovies, bacon, suet, herbs, spice, bread, and eggs, to bind, are a great improvement.

Mrs Elizabeth David, who introduced me to this recipe, considers it a direct ancestor of the Sussex stewed steak which is to be found in her *Spices, Salt and Aromatics in the English Kitchen* (Penguin, 1970). For this you need a 2½ lb piece of chuck steak, top rump or thick flank; a tablespoon or two of flour, 5 to 6 tablespoons each of port and stout, 2 tablespoons of mushroom ketchup or wine vinegar, salt and pepper. Season the meat, and rub flour on both sides, and put it in a shallow baking dish. Slice a large onion over it; pour in the wine, stout, and ketchup or vinegar. Cover with a double sheet of greaseproof paper and the lid of the dish. Cook for about three hours in a very low oven, gas No. 1, 290°F. Serve with mashed potatoes.

GUINNESS STEW

Probably the best-known of beer dishes is *Carbonnades Flamandes*, but experience shows that those who have tried both usually find Guinness stew even better. Ingredients: one large or two small onions; one clove of garlic; dripping; 2½ to 3 lb stewing steak or braising steak cut up into 1½-inch cubes; plain flour, salt, pepper, half a pint of Guinness, one tablespoon vinegar, teaspoon brown sugar, quarter pint beef stock, bouquet garni, stale bread, English or

Dijon mustard. Having melted the sliced onions and garlic in dripping in a frying pan, transfer them to a casserole. Dust the pieces of meat in flour, salt and pepper; fry till brown on all sides, then transfer to casserole. Add a little more dripping to frying-pan and sprinkle ½ oz flour over it. Cook gently for a minute, then gradually add the Guinness, stirring to prevent lumps. Add vinegar, brown sugar and beef stock. Pour the result over the meat and onion, add bouquet garni of thyme, bay leaf and parsley. Cover casserole and cook in low oven (gas Reg. 3). After 2¼ hours take casserole from the oven and place over the top of the stew a layer of thin slices of stale bread spread with mustard. Return the casserole uncovered to the oven for another 30–45 minutes at gas Reg.4 until the bread is crisp on top. Serve with boiled potatoes and bottles of Guinness.

STEAK, KIDNEY AND OYSTER PUDDING

No apologies for another Guinness recipe, since it really is the best for this kind of cooking, and anyway this particular one was put out by the brewery themselves.

1 lb flour, 10 oz finely chopped suet, 1 egg, 1½ lb beef; ½ lb kidney; 4 mushrooms; 3 shallots; a few oysters (the tinned ones will do very well); brown stock; a large wineglassful of Guinness; salt and pepper. Make a paste with the flour, suet, a pinch of salt, the egg and sufficient water to moisten. Line a pudding basin with two-thirds of the paste. Dice the meat and vegetables, sprinkle with salt and pepper and mix well. Fill the basin, and on top of the meat lay a few oysters, with their liquor poured over. Add the Guinness and sufficient stock to moisten thoroughly. Cover the pudding with the remaining paste, press the edges well to seal, cover with greaseproof paper and a pudding cloth tied down tightly. Steam for at least 5 hours, keeping the water on the boil the whole time. Serve by cutting the crust and,

if necessary, removing some of the meat and filling with seasoned brown stock to make more gravy.

TOAD IN THE OLD, OR TOAD IN THE ALE

The name depends on which beer you use. Lightly fry an onion and a pound of sausages, before transferring them to a casserole. Pour on stock and beer in roughly equal quantities until the bangers are slightly more than half submerged. Cover and place in a low-to-medium oven. According to Ben Davis this should be done just before noon opening time on Sunday. Go to the pub for an hour or so. On returning start boiling some potatoes and remove the casserole lid. By the time the spuds are done the top halves of the sausages should be dark and crisp, while the bottom halves will be soft and imbued with the flavour of the liquid. If the sausages are rather fatty, strain off the excess before serving with mashed or boiled potatoes.

JUGGED HARE

Take off the Skin, Quarter it and season it with Pepper, Salt, Mace and Nutmeg. Put it into a Stone Jarr with a Bunch of Thyme, an Onion Stuck with Cloves, a Bay Leaf, half a pint of Gravy, a Quarter of a Pint of Red Wine (or ale is better), tye Down the Jarr very Close. Put it into a Pot of Boiling Water that will cover it to the top. Let it boil four Hours, then take out the Liquor and thicken it with a Brown Cullis. Serve it up in a Soup Dish altogether.

From the MS of Elizabeth Harriet Taylor,
4 September 1779

This is another recipe introduced to me by Mrs Elizabeth David, who found it in *The Surrey Cookery Book*, contributed

to by 58 Women's Institutes, published Guildford 1932.
A 'cullis' or 'coulis' was a concentrated meat stock,
thickened with flour and butter – in fact, the basic brown
sauce.

MUSHROOMS ON TOAST

For two people take ½ lb of mushrooms. Wash them and
remove the stalks (it is quite unnecessary to peel mushrooms).
Brown a chopped garlic clove in 1 oz of butter. Fry the
mushrooms in the butter, adding salt, a little Cayenne
pepper, a dash of Worcestershire sauce and a small wineglass of Guinness. Bring to the boil, and continue to cook
briskly, leaving the pan uncovered, until the sauce is
thickened and reduced. Serve on hot toast.

KIDNEYS ON TOAST

Cut the kidneys into half-inch slices, removing the white
core. Toss them in butter in a frying-pan with a sprinkling
of flour, salt and pepper, stirring well. When the kidneys
have gently browned, add a wineglass of Guinness and
enough stock to cover the kidneys. Cook slowly with the
lid off until the sauce is reduced and the kidneys are tender.
Serve on toast or crisp fried bread. This goes very well with
the above mushroom recipe.

WELSH RABBIT

Beer and cheese are complementary in cooking as at other
times. The best-known combination is of course Welsh
rabbit. Follow common sense and common pronunciation
by calling this dish as above and not Welsh rarebit. The

earliest recorded use of the words Welsh rabbit is 1725; Welsh rarebit is a piece of false etymologizing first recorded sixty years later. Obviously a cheese dish which is called Welsh rabbit is a joke, like Bombay duck (a fish) or a Birmingham screwdriver (a hammer).

To 2 oz of butter add half a pound of grated cheese (Cheddar or Cheshire for preference), $\frac{1}{4}$ cup of beer, salt, pepper, Worcestershire sauce or mustard. Stir till all has melted together (if it's too runny stir in some flour). Pour the result over slices of toast and brown them under the grill.

TAILOR'S DELIGHT

Grated or thinly sliced Double Gloucester is laid at the bottom of a fireproof dish and thinly spread with a good strong mustard (English, Urchfont or Dijon). Cover the cheese with a strong draught bitter or Worthington White Shield and place in a moderate oven till the cheese melts – or achieve the same result in a saucepan over a low heat. When it's all melted, spoon the cheese over slices of toast and pour the warm beer over the top. Sprinkle with red pepper and the result is the kind of thing Ben Gunn used to dream about in his lonely years marooned on Treasure Island.

CAULIFLOWER CHEESE

Trim any ragged or dirty leaves from the cauliflower, and put it in a saucepan of boiling salted water, cooking for 15 minutes or till tender. Drain, and transfer to a casserole. Meanwhile make the sauce: melt a knob of butter in a saucepan and sprinkle a spoonful of flour on to it. Cook for a few seconds, remove from heat and very gradually add $\frac{1}{4}$

pint of light ale to the butter and flour, stirring the whole
time to prevent lumps. When all the beer is added, stir
in 4 oz grated cheese and a goodly dash of Worcestershire
sauce, salt and pepper. Pour the sauce over the colly and
put it at the top of a hot oven or under the grill to brown.

POTTED CHEESE

A delicious way to use up scraps and odds-and-ends of
cheese. Use a hardish English cheese like Cheddar, Cheshire
or Wensleydale, either singly or in combination. Grate the
cheese and add salt, pepper, mustard, Worcestershire
sauce, a pinch of powdered mace and a pinch of Cayenne
pepper. Beat all this together with a lump of butter,
gradually adding a strong ale or barley wine (the exact
amount will depend on how dry the cheese is). When it is
all beaten together to a consistent texture, drink what is
left of the beer. Press the cheese into pots and seal with
melted butter, with a little parsley on top. I find it tastes
better after two or three days, and in a cool place (preferably
not the fridge) it will keep well. Serve on toast or water
biscuits.

GUINNESS CHRISTMAS PUDDING

Ingredients: 10 oz fresh breadcrumbs; 8 oz soft brown sugar;
8 oz currants, 10 oz chopped seeded raisins, 8 oz sultanas,
2 oz chopped mixed peel, 10 oz shredded suet, $\frac{1}{2}$ level
teaspoon salt, 1 level teaspoon mixed spice, grated rind of
one lemon, 1 dessertspoon lemon juice, 2 large eggs, $\frac{1}{4}$
pint milk, $\frac{1}{2}$ pint bottled Guinness.

Mix the dry ingredients together in a large basin. Stir
in lemon juice, beaten eggs, milk and Guinness. Mix well
and turn into one 2-pint and one 3-pint well-greased

pudding basin. Tie pudding cloths over the puddings, or cover them tightly with greaseproof paper and foil. Leave overnight, then steam them for $7\frac{1}{2}$ hours. If not eating the puddings immediately, cool, re-cover and store in a cool place. When required, steam for a further 2–3 hours before serving. This quantity should have enough stopping power to satisfy 12 ordinary people, or 10 greedy ones, or Mr and Mrs Albert Pygge-Strangeways.

PUNCHES, MULLED ALE AND THE LIKE

British beer should normally be served at about 55–60°F. In recent years a bad habit has developed in some places of chilling it, like lager. On the contrary, it is far preferable, particularly in winter, to warm it, especially with the addition of spices or other fortifying agents. Mulling beer, like warming wine, is very simple. Wine snobs make a tremendous business of it, but if you go into a bar in France and ask for *vin chaud* what the barman will probably do is pour out a glass of red wine, put it under the Espresso machine and give it a blast of steam, adding a slice of lemon and a lump of sugar on the way. Similarly, the simplest thing with beer (and the traditional way) is to put a red hot poker in it. For those without red hot pokers a simple method is to pour the beer into a saucepan, add honey or sugar, spices to taste (cloves, cinnamon, ginger, nutmeg) and heat, but *don't boil*. Add a glass of whisky, rum or brandy and you'll be really warm.

Herrick gives the basic recipe for Wassail:

Next crown the bowl full
With gentle Lambs' wool
Add sugar nutmeg and ginger
With store of ale too
And thus ye must do
To make the Wassail a swinger.

Roasted apples, pulped with brown sugar, may be added to a Wassail, or else rings of cooked apple may be floated in the bowl.

Marston, at the end of the sixteenth century, enthused over what sounds like a good punch ('stale' beer was one that had stood long enough to clear, and was usually fairly strong).

> The nut-brown ale, the nut-brown ale,
> Puts down all drink when it is stale:
> The toast, the nutmeg, and the ginger
> Will make a sighing man a singer.
> Ale gives a buffet in the head
>   But ginger under-props the brain;
> When ale would strike a strong man dead
>   Then nutmeg tempers it again.
> The nut-brown ale, the nut-brown ale,
> Puts down all drink when it is stale!

Buttered ale is a concoction of sugar, cinnamon or nutmeg, butter and a lightly hopped beer such as mild. Sometimes beaten egg yolks are also included. A parson in one of Peacock's novels drinks buttered ale as a hangover cure.

In *The Experienced English Housekeeper* (1769) Mrs Elizabeth Raffald gives this recipe for an *Ale Posset*:

To make an Ale Posset.

Put a little white bread in a pint of good milk, set it over the fire then warm a little more than a pint of good strong-ale, with nutmeg and sugar to your taste, then put it in a bowl; when your milk boils pour it upon your ale, let it stand a few minutes to clear, and the curd will rise to the top; then serve it up.

Mrs Raffald and her husband kept the Bull's Head in Manchester market place, and after that the King's Head at Salford. Elizabeth David tells me that there is a story that she had sixteen daughters, and when she died at the age of 48 was working on a book on midwifery.

Huckle-my-buff is a Sussex name for a hot mixture of beer, egg and brandy. *Lamb's wool* is made by mashing roasted apples with a pint of heated brown or old ale to which is added ginger, nutmeg and sugar. Similar mixtures can be made with cloves, raisins, lemons, honey or what you will. Experiment with the ingredients you have available and you'll soon find what suits your taste.

VI The Public House

1 The quest

All the pub's a stage, and all the men and women merely players. Everything about a pub is theatrical: the exits and the entrances, the dialogue, the eating and drinking, the games, the music, the larger-than-life settings from the austerity of the village inn and the public bar to the drawing-room plushness of the saloon bar and the over-magnificence of the gin-palace. Opening time and closing time even give each session the dramatic structure of beginning, middle and end postulated by Aristotle as necessary to a well-made play.

A pub may be calm or boisterous, smart or scruffy, genteel or rough, quiet or noisy, urban or rural, big or small, crowded or empty. No two of the nearly 70,000 in England and Wales are the same. The worst are detestable, the best are unique contributions to human happiness, and among the greatest of British inventions.

A good pub serves two main functions that are distinct but mutually dependent. One is to sell alcoholic drinks for consumption on the premises, and the other is to be a place where social encounters occur. In brief, a pub is a place for social drinking. To use a pub only for drinking or only for socializing is possible but goes against the spirit of the place. You can go to a pub solely to consume alcohol, but in that case you would do better to buy a bottle at an off-licence and take it home to consume by yourself. It is likewise possible to go to the pub for social reasons only and to drink nothing but fruit juice. This is a less serious offence, and for those who have had to forswear alcohol for health or other reasons may be unavoidable. But if everyone were to do this the sociability of the pub would suffer. More volatile people may not need assistance to strike up conversation with strangers. Italians, for example, become extremely agitated on no more than a tiny cup of strong coffee. In colder climates neurotic Swedes and Calvinistic Scots need the help of distilled liquors to release them temporarily from their inhibitions. In most parts of Britain, social intercourse is best lubricated by the moderate consumption of a moderately alcoholic drink – beer.

A few pubs are hostile. They are easily spotted and should be avoided. In most it takes only two or three visits to be accepted as a regular, the status of full membership being achieved when you can go in and ask for 'the usual'. This enormously comfortable phrase is characteristic of a good pub, which is a place where you should feel welcome, a place for meeting people of all kinds on terms of equality and in an atmosphere of tolerance and conviviality.

About thirty years ago George Orwell wrote a description of his favourite pub. It was in a quiet side-street and its name was The Moon Under Water. The customers were mostly regulars who went there not only for the beer (which was good) but also for the conversation. The Moon Under Water was rich in that indefinable quality called 'atmosphere', and this came at least in part from the uncompromisingly Victorian architecture and fittings. There were no glass-topped tables or 'other modern miseries' (the equivalent today would be Formica), 'no sham roof-beams, ingle-nooks or plastic panels masquerading as oak'. Instead there was plenty of grained woodwork, ornamental mirrors, cast-iron fireplaces and a florid ceiling stained to a yellowy-brown by years of tobacco-smoke, all combining to produce what Orwell called 'the solid comfortable ugliness of the nineteenth century'.

The Moon Under Water had games, in particular darts (in the public bar). There was no radio or piano, so it was always quiet enough to talk. The barmaids knew most of the customers by name, or else called them 'Dear' (irrespective of age or sex). There were always snacks available, and on weekdays you could buy a good, solid cooked lunch for a price that was less than you would pay for a comparable meal in a restaurant. The Moon Under Water had a delightful garden. In summer you could take your drink outside and sit under the plane trees, and at one end of the garden there were swings and a slide where the children could play.

The Moon Under Water didn't exist. Orwell was playing a variation on an old and well-loved English game which is the quest for the perfect pub. Having failed to find it Orwell invented one. The perfect pub will never be found. It is the drinker's Shangri-la. Some dedicated amateurs devote their entire lives to searching for it. They travel all over the country, sampling local beers, exploring unknown pubs. It will never be found, partly because if someone thought he had discovered it no one else would agree, and partly because, if he and they did, it would be the end of the game.

Orwell's essay has the merit of identifying the most important components that constitute the conviviality of a good pub – the people, the drink, the food, the talk, the games, the music, the design. Let us take these one at a time.

2 The people

Whining schoolboys and infants mewling and puking in their mothers' arms are to be found only in a few remote pubs in unpoliced areas, but the other five of Jaques's seven ages of man are readily identified among pub regulars – the young lovers; the soldier full of strange oaths, 'sudden and quick in quarrel'; the round-bellied solid citizen 'full of wise saws and modern instances'; the lean and slippered pantaloon; and finally the very old man in the corner of the public bar taking all evening over his bottle of Brown in 'second childishness and mere oblivion; Sans teeth, sans eyes, sans taste, sans everything.'

There is no evidence that Shakespeare was thinking of the regulars in his local when he put these words into Jaques's mouth. There is equally no evidence that he was not. We know that the Bard was a keen pubman, and in the regulars of the Boar's Head Tavern, Eastcheap, in the *Henry IV* plays he presents many characters that are still recognizable pub types. Falstaff, Poins, red-nosed Bardolph, Peto, Gadshill, Mistress Quickly – all have their modern counterparts. Prince Hal, for example, was the young blood out slumming. Today he is a young stockbroker taking his King's Road girl friend to an East End pub that puts on drag shows. In the country he's a young man called Roger who goes to agricultural college, wears a flat cap and cavalry twill trousers, drives a sports car, talks too loud and has a girl friend called Jennifer who wears a headscarf.

Falstaff is the pub wit. T. E. B. Clarke, whose book *What's Yours?*, published in 1938, remains one of the best guides to publand, calls this character the Chief 'One'. He is 'master of backchat, indefatigable collector of doubtful stories, fervent and thoroughly frank admirer of barmaids – in short, a cackle-creator without compare – this character is one of the pub's most priceless assets.' At their worst pub wits can be real bores, compulsively telling jokes which are relentlessly sexual or racial. Some of them may strike you as hilarious on the first two or three encounters, after which they begin to induce a feeling of extreme weariness. Conversation ceases as the listener becomes first audience, then victim. You become tongue-tied. Every remark you make seems more leaden than the previous one, as the wag plays you like a matador with a bull, while you are unwillingly cast in the role of straight man or feed.

But once or twice in a lifetime the assiduous pub explorer will come across a wit of real genius, a man like Falstaff who can tell a story, or make an observation, or slam back repartee with such adroitness as to shake the laughter out of you whether you want to laugh or not.

T. E. B. Clarke's typology includes such characters as The Same-Again Man and The Major who are both still to be found in most pubs. The Major may never actually have held that rank, or even never have been a soldier: it is enough for him to be a sprightly but elderly gentleman with a white moustache, an erect bearing and, Clarke suggests, 'a few military habits – such as coming smartly to attention on entering the bar and saluting the company with a shouldered umbrella'.

The Pub Bore is another who will always be with us. Clarke sees him as a failed wit, a pathetic case whose ambition is to supplant the Chief 'One'. I see him quite differently, as a monomaniac. He is boring on only one subject, but such is the nature of his illness that he is unable to keep off that subject for more than a few minutes. His obsession can take almost any form. A common case is the man who insists on giving you a blow-by-blow account of his holiday in Spain, detailing precisely what each member of his family ate at every meal, what his wife said, the price, and the digestive consequences.

Then there's the Why-my-wife-left-me bore, the Send-them-back-to-Ireland/West Indies bore, and the useless information bore. The drinks bore is one of the worst, taking you back over his Greatest Nights Out: 'I'd had two large Pernods at the club for a start, then a quick pint at the station, when I met Ian and Dave, and I said I've just got time for a quick one and he insisted on brandy, large ones mind, and if we had one we had five, and then we went to a spaghetti place and we must have had three bottles of Chianti or more like four, and then Dave said

I've got a bottle of Scotch at my place, so we picked up Sheila and Brenda who had a bottle of Cointreau and . . .'

Commonest of all in our economic climate is the inflation bore, the deadliest of the species being the When-I-was-a-lad variety: 'When I was a lad, mind you this is going back let me see now thirty, no, more like thirty-five years, you could go out for the evening, take your girl with you, slap-up meal with all the trimmings, two cinema tickets, best seats, four pints of beer, you're not old enough to remember this but beer was beer in those days, not like this piss, and how much do you think that little lot would have cost?'

'I have no idea,' you say.

'Go on, have a guess,' he insists.

'Eightpence.'

'No, be serious. How much do you think?'

The situation is hopeless. He will not release you until you have exposed yourself to his ridicule by naming a figure well in excess of the one he has in mind.

'Two quid,' you sigh.

'Two quid!' the swine exclaims. 'Hey, Fred, did you hear that? Two quid! You could have had all that and a bus home and still have enough change from ten bob for a packet of fags.'

It is obvious he is lying, but all you can do is murmur 'Really?'

'And I'll tell you another thing.'

'I'm sure you will.'

'We were a damn sight better off in those days.'

And so on.

A benefit of rising petrol costs has been a slight decline in car bores. Regrettably, recent years have seen the emergence of a new breed, the beer bore. Readers of this book, who certainly do not number among them, will equally certainly have met them. It is not their enthusiasm for real beer that is objectionable. On the contrary it is admir-

able. It is rather that they are apparently interested in, and
can talk about, nothing else but beer and carbon dioxide,
and they insist on imposing their views and (usually
inaccurate) information on all within earshot. At their very
worst, groups of beer bores form into herds that roam the
country in search of inoffensive pubs where the beer is not
of the approved kind, and then proceed to bully the landlord
and customers. Such behaviour is intolerable.

There are two ways of handling pub bores. One is to
escape to another bar (this is one of the arguments in favour
of a pub having more than one bar). The other is to
become a bore-spotter. The specimens described above are
offered as a tentative first step towards working out a
Linnaean system of bore-classification. Remember, however, that it is essential to proceed with *extreme caution*.
In attempting to become a bore-spotter you may well
contract the disease yourself. This is the kind of risk that
scientists have always had to take.

Classic women pub characters have in the past been
limited to the peroxide lady drinking Gin-and-It in the
saloon bar, and the old dears with their port-and-lemon
in the public. Fortunately far more women now use pubs.
A wider selection of drinks, food, increasing economic
independence and the erosion of male supremacy have all
contributed to this welcome development. There is still a
long way to go. In the north of England there are still
bars that are in effect all-male, and even in the south most
women will only go alone to a pub they know extremely
well. One deterrent is the women's lavatories, which sound
even less congenial than most Gents.

Unless and until the recommendations of the Erroll
Committee (1972) are implemented children are excluded
from the pub's *dramatis personae*. The purpose of the law
as it stands is to protect young people from possibly harmful
environments. The Erroll Report recommends that children

should be admitted to some pubs or parts of pubs. This would at least do away with the pathetic sight of the family out for a drive who stop for a snack at a pub, when father has to trudge to and from the car park with sandwiches and glasses of lemonade. Since it usually rains at weekends the scene is made yet more heart-rending.

It is true that admitting children would alter the character of the pub, but in my view it would be a change for the better. Like the increasing use of pubs by women, it would be another step away from the concept of the pub as a place for men to go and get drunk together. The disappearance of such pubs, which still exist in urban areas and in the north of England and Scotland, would be entirely beneficial. The wife who stays at home preparing Sunday lunch has already begun to ask why she too shouldn't go to the pub. Why shouldn't the children go as well and make it a family outing?

Some of the best pubs already admit children. They are usually country pubs which to some extent double as village shop, so that kids are forever popping in and out to buy milk or eggs for mum, sweets or crisps for themselves, or baccy for granddad. If anything the presence of children has a sobering effect. Alcohol is more likely to be abused when bought and sold in an atmosphere of furtiveness (as in Sweden, which has a high rate of alcoholism) than when it is accepted as a normal part of social life and diet (as in Italy, which has a low rate).

After this brief discussion of customers let us turn to those who spend their lives behind bars. We will begin with the livestock. In many pubs there are enormous animals which the owner will tell you are alsatians or Lithuanian elk-hounds or some such breed of dog. In fact they are untamed wolves and should be treated with respect, especially by burglars and other villains with ambitions concerning the Saturday night takings. There is no objection to a publican keeping a pack of these beasts if they are kept out of sight. If they venture into the drinking area it is a different matter.

Cats are good pub animals but are better at sleeping in front of the fire than at deterring criminal elements. Budgerigars are not bad pub animals, but the repetitive conversation of the mynah bird makes it unsuitable. At the Bell, Aldworth, a chicken called Henrietta used to stroll through when the doors were left open: after she grew a comb and started crowing her name was changed to Henry. At the Catherine Wheel, Goring-on-Thames, a bag of nuts hangs outside the window: on the rare occasions when conversation flags you can watch the foraging tits. Mr Leslie Symes of the Mendip Inn, Gurney Slade, kept hedgehogs at one time and planned to hold the first ever European Hedgehog Championship. He trained them on bitter: 'Hedgehogs drink beer like one o'clock,' he told me. Unfortunately when the contestants came out of hibernation in the spring they started mating and fighting one another and Mr Symes had to let them go. When last heard of they were living wild somewhere at the bottom of his garden.

Now for the humans behind the bar. Barmaids are rather rare birds nowadays. Their traditional physical attribute is buxomness (Buxom: full of health, vigour, and good temper: plump and comely, 'jolly' – *Shorter Oxford Dictionary*). The girl serving at the bar at the Folies Bergères in Manet's painting is far too soulful and sulky to make a good barmaid. She should be down-to-earth, boundlessly cheerful, unsubtly erotic, a sympathetic listener with a stinging line in repartee for dealing with cheeky customers. Sometimes they have a laugh which endangers the wine-glasses but this is not necessary. T. E. B. Clarke observed nearly forty years ago that most barmaids are called Ruby and usually come from Portsmouth. Nowadays they are either called Mary and come from Limerick or else

Sue and come from Melbourne.

Barmen and barmaids are to some extent a dying race, except in very large pubs. With labour costs always rising pubs are increasingly run by the licensee and spouse alone. Licensee is a horrid word, but sometimes unavoidable. Landlord is often inaccurate, tenants and managers too discriminatory, and for some reason publicans don't like being called publicans (perhaps it's the association with sinners). Mine Host suggests Olde Worlde British Travel and Holiday Association advertisements. Perhaps the best word is the usual London term, the guvnor (possibly spelt guv'nor, but never governor). It has none of the disadvantages of the other words and also conveys some sense of the massive authority of this important person. There's no reason why women licensees should not also be given this name. To call them governesses would convey entirely inappropriate suggestions of kinkiness.

The guvnor has not changed significantly since Chaucer described him in *The Canterbury Tales*. The host of the Tabard, Southwark, was a solid citizen, forthright, sensible, well-informed, genial, slightly long-winded, a tactful arbitrator, all things to all men, laughing at jokes, settling disputes, organizing games and outings. The female guvnor was pinned down by Shakespeare in the form of the sprightly and motherly Mistress Quickly in the *Henry IV* and *Henry V* plays. Many of the best guvnors are women, but most guvnors are men, so for reasons of economy I shall refer to the guvnor and his wife, but would like the alternative of guvnor and her husband to be understood.

The character of a pub depends on the guvnor more than anything else. Like the schoolmaster in the classroom he is both referee and focal point of attention. The skill with which he looks after the beer is of prime importance to the connoisseur, but everyone is affected by the atmosphere he and his wife generate through their conversation, and the type of custom they encourage or discourage. Their taste in interior decoration, their instinctive sense of traditional pub design, the knick-knacks and souvenirs they collect on their holidays, create the visual mood of the pub.

The guvnor usually avoids conversation on topics such as politics and religion where passions may run high. The tenant landlord, like such other self-employed people as taxi-drivers, barbers and tobacconists, tends to be conservative. He is often Conservative as well. In private he may reveal himself as positively reactionary. The *Morning Advertiser*, the newspaper of the licensed victuallers, carries almost daily reports, speeches, letters or editorials calling for the restoration of national service and corporal or capital punishment. The guvnor hates strikers and VAT collectors just about equally. Surprisingly often he is teetotal. Some licensees are heavy drinkers; most are steady but moderate in consumption, often of bottled Guinness.

Customers should remember that the pub is the guvnor's house, and usually his home, and should behave like guests. American visitors should not bark their habitual 'Gimme a beer': they are more likely to warm him by some such approach as 'Good evening, I'd like a pint of your excellent bitter, if I may.' The illusion should be maintained as far as possible that you are dropping in on a friend, and the financial transactions should be conducted with minimum comment. The guvnor is anything but a waiter. You are on his premises and should treat him with due respect. He is as good a man as you and quite probably better. And when you leave, don't forget to say goodnight.

About one pub in five is a Free House. This means that the landlord is precisely that: he owns the pub and can sell beer from whatever brewery he chooses. Tied Houses are owned by brewers, and about three-quarters of them are tenanted, and a quarter managed. A manager is paid a straight salary, whereas a tenant runs his own business with the restriction that he has to buy beer and other drinks from the owning brewery.

In recent years considerable ill-feeling has been caused by the big brewers' policy of switching pubs from tenancies to management. This policy was started by Watney's, who started giving notice to London tenants in the early 1970s, an example that was followed by the other big companies. It can be argued (and the Brewers' Society does so argue) that it is not really the concern of the customer whether a house is tenanted or managed: the issue is one solely between the licensees and the brewers. What is important to the customer is whether the pub is run well or badly. There are some excellent managed pubs and some horrible tenanted ones. This is all true, but in practice the best pubs seem to be tenanted and the best tenanted pubs are better than the best managed ones. To take just one example, there is every difference between a managed pub which has been given some 'theme' by the clowns in the brewers' design department and turned into a Swiss chalet or a Wild West saloon, and a pub which houses a collection of beer mugs, weapons, farm implements or railwayana assembled by the guvnor himself, on which he may have expert knowledge and be able to talk interestingly and at length.

The big brewers argue that there are particular cases where only a manager is suitable. This is occasionally true. In fact, though, the deciding factor is which system makes the brewers most money. This became apparent when rent restrictions were lifted early in 1975, since which time the brewers have in some cases found it profitable to switch back from management to tenancies.

3 The talk

The purpose of pub conversation is to find areas of agreement and common ground. Confrontation and controversy are usually avoided. *Pub and the People*, Mass Observation's pre-war study of the pubs of 'Worktown' (in fact Bolton), listed the following topics of pub conversation: betting, sport, work, people, drinking, weather, politics and 'dirt'. These seem to be fairly universal and not to have changed much, but the topic is less important than the way it is treated. Indeed, the accomplished pubman can conduct a perfectly satisfactory conversation without a topic at all. If you can't manage that, try to remember not to leap straight into a subject without going through elaborate preliminaries. First you must announce your presence. 'Hullo Fred, good evening Jim' you say (unless it happens to be eleven o'clock in the morning). Next comes the buying of the drink. If you are a regular and know most of the other customers someone may offer to buy this for you. The convention always used to be that the newcomer's drink was bought by the person who was lucky enough to get there first: if you offered to buy him a drink he would then correctly counter with the words 'No, no, I'm in the chair'. Nowadays I'm afraid he may well reply 'Thank you very much'. The usual offer nowadays is 'What'll you have?' 'What's yours?' is not as common as it used to be, and 'What's your poison?' is now rare.

The accomplished pubman will always name his drink without hesitation. If he is on home ground this is easy, particularly if he has been making the same order several times a day for eighteen years. However, he should be able to show just as much confidence on an away match. Wild inspection of the pumps will establish you as a stranger, and therefore an object of derision, every bit as much as those Americans who give pubmen so much innocent delight by asking for a glass of beer. For those whose normal request is for a pint of mild or bitter and who find themselves facing nothing but chromium taps foaming at the mouth with fizzy keg beer, the correct order is a bottle of Guinness or a White Shield Worthington.

If your drink is part of a round then it is churlish to lift

it straight to your lips without the courtesy of a quietly
murmured toast. In the past there was a wide variety from
which to choose: Down the Hatch, Mud in your Eye,
My Best Respects, Chin Chin, and many others. Most of
these seem largely to have disappeared, let alone such
exotic toasts as the pre-war 'Fluff in your latchkey' and the
1920s' 'Long Legs to the Baby.' Nowadays 'Cheers' is
probably the most widespread toast, though Cheerio,
Good Luck and Your Very Good Health are still often
heard.

Now for the opening moves in the conversation. The
weather is always safe provided you don't get technical
about it. In sub-zero conditions in February, a remark like
'Not a bit like summer, is it?' will be received much better
than meteorological observations about cold fronts, anti-
cyclones and alto-cumulus clouds. It always goes down well
to say that you don't know why you bother to listen to
the weather forecast, they always get it wrong.

If there's a pub dog or cat, an inquiry about its age,
breed or health is a sound follow-up. You can thus gradually
work your way towards a topic, or an anecdote about the
latest exploit of some local character, or a reminiscence about
what happened on the way back from the darts match.
If the pub wit is there, let him make the running. Be prepared to be interrupted just as you are reaching the punch-
line of your favourite joke: the guvnor may be called away
to serve another customer, or some other regular may
arrive, which means that the whole process has to start all
over again at 'Good evening Jim, Hullo Fred'.

A perennial subject is drinks. Brewers have been complained about throughout history, and nowadays moaning
at the bar is as vigorous as ever. Like other sports this one
has expanded enormously in recent years and become
much better organized. In the old days a player could go to
his pub and run down (or, very rarely, up) the local beer
in comparison with that of the North/South/neighbouring

county/Spain/Germany on the basis of nothing more than
pure prejudice. A classic comment (one which has enjoyed
something of a revival recently) is to say that such-and-such
a beer is like making love in a punt (fucking near water).
There was one ploy which above all others represented the
peak of achievement for a player of the old school. He
would sit in a pub for weeks, months, years if necessary,
as patient as an angler, waiting for someone to remark that
'It looks like rain'. He would then slowly and solemnly
raise his glass of beer and murmur 'With just a faint taste
of hops'.

The modern school can rarely match the elegance of such
play. Today the rapier has been replaced by the bludgeon
of facts and figures about original gravities, hopping rates,
means of dispense and such prosaic details (see Chapter 3).
The new style was developed in response to the crisis in
which real beer (whether good or bad) appeared to be in
danger of disappearing altogether. Some observers regret
the element of professionalism that has entered the game,
but there was an emergency on and it is hard to see what
else could have been done.

Still, all pubmen are brothers under the skinful, and not
even such a tentative account of pub talk as this one can
ignore the richness of vocabulary for describing the condition brought on by excessive consumption of alcohol.
This very rarely makes people drunk. Instead it renders
them jarred, jugged, bottled, pickled, bevvied, steamin',
plonked, smashed, flutered, high, tanked, mortal, steam-
boats, sloshed, tiddly, under the influence, tired and emo-
tional, half cut, well away, high as a kite, pissed as a newt,
stotious, and tight as an owl. Such people have had a few,
had enough, got a few inside them. They have drink taken.
Roget's *Thesaurus* offers such euphemisms and synonyms as
tipsy, inebriated, in one's cups, in a state of intoxication,
fuddled, mellow, boozy, fresh, merry, elevated, squiffy,
befuddled, sozzled, flushed, groggy, beery, top-heavy, pot-

valiant, overcome, screwed, tight, primed, oiled, muddled, muzzy, bosky, obfuscated, maudlin, dead-drunk, blind-drunk, the worse for liquor, having had a drop too much, half seas over, three sheets in the wind, under the table, blind to the world, one over the eight, drunk as a lord, drunk as an owl, bibacious, bibulous and sottish.

The Waterdrinkers, Norman Longmate's entertaining history of the temperance movement, quotes from *The Drunkard Opened*, 1635, such terms as 'He is foxt, he is flustered, he is subtle, he hath seen the French king, he hath swallowed a tavern-token, he hath whipt the cat, he hath been at the scriveners, he is bit by a barn-weasel.'

The best-known Cockney rhyming-slang term is probably elephants, being short for elephant's trunk, but there are also all the musical terms – Chopin and Liszt, Mozart and Liszt, Brahms and Liszt – and solo whist, elbows and wrist, and of course Isle of Wight.

Further terms, compiled out of a great many letters received from readers of the *Guardian* who rose nobly to the challenge, include: pallatic, paralytic, legless, miraculous, langerred, blotto, plastered, stoned, *entre deux vins*, stewed, zonked, blathered, foul, rotten, shickered, stonkered, full as a frog, mouldy, bullifants, bollixed, taking both sides of the road, bevvied, drunk as a sack, tight as a drum, pie-eyed, sloshed, sozzled, fuzzled, full as a boot, fu', pissed as a handcart, pissed as a rat, pissed as a skunk, pissed as a fart, pissed as arseholes, in a muckin' fuddle, pixielated, under the weather and peeshed. Finally, Mr W. Yates of Henley-in-Arden tells me that the Manchester police used to book people whom they described as being 'drunk and refusing to fight', and also reminds me of an exchange that took place once when F. E. Smith was pleading in court.

Smith: I contend that at the time my client was as drunk as a judge.

Judge: My learned friend should know that the expression

is 'As drunk as a Lord'.

Smith (bowing slightly): As Your Lordship pleases.

4 The drinks

The main one is of course beer, or in the West country cider. Wine and spirits are sold increasingly, but with fluctuations according to the time of the day, the day of the week, the season of the year, the weather and the nation's economy. When buying spirits in a pub remember that if you simply ask for whisky or gin you will probably get the brewery's house brand, which may well not be the best. If you are particular, then specify Bell's, Teacher's or whatever is your favourite dram. Some circumspection is also needed when buying wine. In most pubs it is plonk, and they sell so little that when it is finally finished, days after being opened, it may be getting a bit rough. Some pubs make a speciality of wine, in which case you may have better luck. Almost certainly the best pub for wine is the Toastmaster's Inn, Burham, near Maidstone, Kent: the astounding wine list has 150 clarets alone.

Many people like to mix beer either with another kind of beer or with some altogether different drink. Some mixtures are well-known, such as shandy (lemonade or ginger beer with bitter or mild) and lager-and-lime. Black Velvet, a mixture of Guinness and champagne, enjoys a high reputation but seems to me to be less pleasurable than either of the ingredients on its own. Here are some other familiar drink mixtures:

Black and tan: stout and bitter, sometimes stout and mild.

Mother-in-law: Old and bitter.

Boilermaker: Brown and mild.

M and B: Mild and bitter.

Narfer narf: Half a pint of mild and half a pint of bitter. Half a pint of this mixture is called *narfer narfer narf*.

Happy Days: in Dunbar this name is given to a half of bitter and a wee heavy.

Dragon's Blood: Barley wine and rum.

Dog's nose: Bitter and gin. This is better than it sounds, though rarely made now as it was in Dickens's day. *The Pickwick Papers* contains a report of the committee of the Brick Lane Branch of the United Grand Junction Ebenezer Temperance Association:

> Your committee have pursued their grateful labours during the past month, and have the unspeakable pleasure of reporting the following additional cases of converts to Temperance.
>
> H. Walker, tailor, wife and two children. When in better circumstances owns to having been in the constant habit of drinking ale and beer; says he is not certain whether he did not twice a week, for twenty years, taste 'dog's nose', which your committee find upon enquiry, to be compounded of warm porter, moist sugar, gin, and nutmeg (a groan, and 'So it is!' from an elderly female).

Lightplater: light and bitter.

Granny: Old and mild.

Blacksmith: barley wine and Guinness.

Port and Guinness: port and Guinness.

The above are all fairly established mixtures and in varying degrees pleasant. There are also some revolting concoctions that are widespread, to say nothing of those that are ordered out of sheer bravado. Blackcurrant is the most widespread pollutant and I have received reports from all over the country of such horrors as lager and blackcurrant, mild and blackcurrant, and bitter and blackcurrant. In the interests of pure research I ordered the last of these at my local. The landlord went white but poured it like a man. It looked like ox-blood, and the one sip I took was indescribably sweet and sickly.

In Liverpool I have seen Guinness and blackcurrant being drunk with apparent pleasure, and I have eyewitness reports of Guinness and lime, Guinness and orange, Guinness and Coke, Guinness and Advokaat (my God), Guinness and tomato juice, and Guinness and Vimto.

Other assorted vilenesses: gin and milk; Pernod and cider; Pernod, lime, blackcurrant and Benedictine; cider and tomato juice; brandy and blackcurrant. There's a pub in Wales where after hours the guvnor and his cronies used to compete at making the nastiest possible drink from the bottles on the shelves: the winner was a mixture of Hollands gin and the juice from a jar of cockles. Much better than it sounds is milk and Mackeson (or other sweet stout). For a knockout mixture I recommend a Fast Lady (gin and Campari).

5   The food

Only about ten years ago pub food rarely went beyond crisps, pickled eggs and sandwiches which were bought second-hand from British Railways. Nowadays most pubs will offer a fairly substantial range of snacks, and (especially in the towns of the south) hot meals at a price well below that of any restaurant. Nowadays nearly 10 per cent of all food consumed outside the home is bought in pubs.

Pub sandwiches are almost invariably made with tasteless and indigestible pre-sliced bread. For this reason it is usually better to have a roll or French bread which are usually closer approximations to the real thing. The ubiquitous 'Ploughman's' – bread, butter, cheese, pickled onions – represents the best and worst of pub food. If it's real bread and mature farmhouse Cheddar then there's nothing better. All too often the cheese is the mass-produced creamery product that masquerades under the name of Cheddar: immature, rindless and tasteless.

Peanuts are popular and pleasant, but the classic pub food remains the potato crisp. Frank Smith founded his crisp business in Cricklewood in 1920 with a staff of twelve. Two years later this great man had the idea of putting little twists of salt-filled blue paper into the packets, which were then delivered in airtight tins by large blue vans all over the country. Though there were many local competitors Smith's prospered mightily. It was the national crisp, and the Smith's crisp empire appeared impregnable. Then came Golden Wonder which, with energetic marketing and many strange-flavoured crisps, carried all before it. Smith's was soon outstripped and, once proudly independent, was acquired by General Mills Inc. of Minneapolis in 1965. At about the same time the little blue twists of salt disappeared.

Ten years later, at the beginning of 1975, Smith's brought out Salt 'n' Shake – plain crisps with a little bag of salt inside. This was a shrewd bid for the nostalgia market, and seems to have paid off. Unfortunately the salt is now in what looks like a tea-bag: the original machines had disappeared and the hand-twisters had all retired. The modern version has a bag of salt in each packet, whereas there should be none in some and several in others (if you're going in for nostalgia you have to get the details right). Also the bags of salt are at the top of the packet, whereas they should lurk at the bottom waiting to be discovered when there's only one crisp left. Finally the new bags are airtight, which means that the salt is not soggy as it should be.

Crisps are an extremely expensive way of buying cold fried potatoes; they work out at somewhere around £1 a pound. However they are great fun to eat, the pleasure in tearing open the packet and the crunching noise made when eating them being just as important as the taste or nutritional value. Otherwise we would have been collectively bonkers to have bought 3,000 million packets in 1974 (a third Smith's, slightly more Golden Wonder) at a cost of £112 million.

In the view of most connoisseurs, the best crisps now are Walkers' of Thurmaston, Leicester, to be found mostly in pubs in the Midlands, Yorkshire, and Anglia. As well as being delicate in shape, taste and colour the packets carry interesting facts culled from the *Guinness Book of Records* which may make useful conversational talking-points (see above). As I write the most recent packet of Walkers' Crisps I have bought informs me that the largest dish in the world is roasted camel: this is sometimes offered at Bedouin wedding feasts. To make it, all you have to do is stuff cooked eggs into fish, the fish into cooked chickens, the chickens into a whole roasted sheep, and the sheep into a camel.

6 The games

Games have always been closely associated with pubs, though often in the face of official disapproval. The very first regulations for national control of premises on which alcoholic liquor is sold appear in Henry VII's statute of 1495, and are aimed at discouraging the indoor games which were distracting Tudor pubmen from archery.

Many pub names are taken from the games and sports with which they were once associated, and very unpleasant some of them have been too. The Cock, The Cockpit, The Fighting Cocks; The Bull; The Fox and Hounds; The Hare and Hounds; The Dog and Duck: such names testify that these were once pubs for cock-fighting, bull-baiting, fox-hunting, hare-coursing and duck-baiting (pinioned ducks were released over a pond and customers and their dogs competed to catch them). In the eighteenth and nineteenth centuries ratting was carried out on a huge scale in pubs with the necessary pits. Mayhew mentions a publican who bought 26,000 live rats a year. Intensive betting went on about which dog could kill the most in the shortest time.

There are still many boxing, horse-racing and football pubs. The Jockey Club was founded in an inn, and cricket started as a pub game. Richard Nyren, the publican of The Bat and Ball at Hambleden, played a crucial part in the early history of cricket. In those heroic days this small village took on the rest of England no fewer than 29 times – and won. There aren't many pubs with their own cricket or football pitches, but for these outdoor games the local is still essential for displaying fixture lists and trophies, refreshing players before and after the match, and for analysing what went wrong during the rest of the week.

Amongst its many functions the local is a sports and leisure centre, and games are an essential part of its convivial and socializing work. The diversity of pub games is enormous – from darts, with its combined skills of eye, hand and mental arithmetic, to the low cunning of Spoof. The best games have three characteristics in common. First, they can give great pleasure to beginners, and it is also possible to develop a high degree of skill at them. Second, they can be played by a variable number of people. Third, they involve only small sums of money – at most the price of a round of drinks. The classic pub games – darts, dominoes, shove-ha'penny – all score highly by these criteria. The fruit machine or one-armed bandit is an unsociable and solitary game, requiring no skill, and is also extremely expensive: in short, a bad pub game on all counts.

Darts is the most popular of pub games. It may have originated in knife-throwing or some form of indoor archery using the end of a cask as the target. The archery theory receives some support from the fact that in London the darts are still called arrows – or, more correctly, 'arrers'. Darts only achieved real popularity in this century, developing into a national craze between the wars, and unfortunately sweeping out many older and localized games in the process. By the time of the Second World War the game had achieved such popularity that when Marmaduke A. Breckon beat Jim Pike at the Agricultural Hall, Islington, in 1939 he did so in front of a crowd of nearly 20,000. There are now reckoned to be some six or seven million regular players in the British Isles. There are a million registered league players, 750,000 of them being competition players. This means that darts surpasses even angling as the biggest participator sport in the country.

Until 1908 the legality of darts in pubs was in some doubt as it had not been established whether it was a game of skill or chance. Tom Barrett (himself twice winner of the *News of the World* Championship) describes in his book *Darts* (Pan, 1973) how the issue was settled by the Leeds Magistrates Court. A landlord called 'Foot' Anakin was prosecuted for allowing a game of chance, darts, to be played on his licensed premises. 'Foot' asked for permission to give a demonstration, and a dart board was brought into court. The highest number on the board is a twenty, and 'Foot' threw three of them. A junior clerk of the court was invited to try and missed the board altogether with two of his darts. The magistrates asked 'Foot' if he could repeat the performance. Now the highest possible score with one dart is not the bull (50) but the treble twenty (60). This is an area rather smaller than the edge of a matchbox. 'Foot's' first dart was a treble twenty, as was his second, and his third. The magistrate was satisfied. Darts is not a game of chance.

When players reach that level of skill they sometimes make things more difficult for themselves by playing with sharpened hairpins or six-inch nails, but for you or me (well, me anyway) the ordinary game is quite hard enough. The conventional board and the games of 301, or 501, or 1001, starting and ending with a double, are too familiar

to need describing here. There are variants on the standard
board, though, that deserve a mention. In the East End
of London, Southwark, and just into Kent and Suffolk,
you may come across a Fives board, which is divided into
areas scoring 5, 10, 15 and 20. There are other variations,
such as the Yorkshire board, which has no treble or outer
bull, and the distance of throw varies from London's
nine feet to Nottingham's mere six (surprisingly it doesn't
make much difference).

The most intimidating board is the Log-end, Manchester
or Lancashire board. It presents a much smaller target
than the conventional one. In the usual game on this board,
Round the Clock, you have to end by hitting a particular
double which is about the size of a matchstick, and then
the Bull, which is about the size of the head of a carpet-tack.
It makes the standard dart-board look cissy.

If you find it hard to hit the part of the board you are
aiming at try at least to learn the language of the game. A
few useful phrases are:

Middle for diddle: the player who throws the dart nearest
the centre of the board starts the game.

Mugs away: the loser of the previous game starts.

Front room: a close game, nothing in it (like our front
room).

Away: in the standard game this means you have hit a
double and your score now begins to count.

Bust, or over: at the end of the standard game this means
you have scored more than is needed.

There are often local variations for the names of numbers.
Thus: Harry's Eye or Annie's Room is 1. Two Little Ducks,
or Swans on the Lake is 22; half a crown is 26; All the
Varieties is obviously 57; 76 is Trombones; and Ton is 100.

If your score stands at 257 and you throw a treble 17,
a 9 and a 7 it will impress no one if you add up on your
fingers – three seventeens are 51, and 9 is 60, and 7 is 67.
It will cut even less ice if you write 67 under the 257,

draw a line under it and then subtract. The skilled darts player's arithmetic is as swift as an arrer. Try to get your opponent to do the scoring.

Second to darts among pub games is dominoes. Dominoes probably originated in China thousands of years ago, but were only introduced to England by French prisoners-of-war in the eighteenth century. The pieces are traditionally made of ebony with an ivory inlay, but man-made materials are beginning to replace them. The standard set, numbered from double blank to double six, consists of 28 pieces, though in the north-west of England the set goes up to double 9, and elsewhere reportedly they go even higher. Dominoes players are men of few words and deep thoughts. Unlike swimming, where world records are made by thirteen-year-olds, dominoes is a game for the late developer, with players reaching peak form in their early seventies.

Associated with dominoes, because they usually share the same scoring-board, is cribbage. According to John Aubrey this card game was invented by the remarkable Cavalier poet, wit and gambler, Sir John Suckling. Having invented cribbage he sent marked packs of cards before him in his progress round the country. By this means he made £20,000: the equivalent today would probably be £2 million. He died in poverty, having gambled the lot away, doubtless on games that were not of his own invention played with cards that were not marked – at least by him.

In various parts of the country particular local card games are allowed to be played for small stakes by specific permission of the licensing magistrates. Cribbage enjoys the distinction of being the one and only card game allowed under the 1968 Gaming Act to be played for small stakes in pubs throughout the country.

Fairly rare, but to my mind the most delightful of all pub games, is shove-ha'penny. There is a delicately sensuous pleasure in the silent slide of the coin across the glass-like polish of the wood or powdered slate, ending in the tiniest of clicks as it strikes another coin. Virtuosi can perform wonders at this game, swinging the path of the coin and adroitly ricocheting the coins into position. On a really polished board it is even possible to make a coin bounce back on hitting another. A score of five with five coins is called a Gold Watch.

This brief survey is not concerned with rules (they are usually best acquired on the spot from regulars) but I will make a small exception here. The winner in shove-ha'penny is the player who first places three coins in each of the nine transverse spaces ('beds'). How do you decide if a coin is in, or if it is just touching the line? Some boards have sunken brass dividing-lines that can be raised to see if they move the coin or not. Some players run the edge of a piece of paper or the blade of a knife or engineering feelers between the coin and the line. This is poor stuff. The rule is that the coin must not only be in, it must be clearly seen to be in. If you have to ask the scorer for a decision, then it's out. A good player will never argue the issue.

This delightful game, which dates from Tudor times, is to be found mostly in the south of England, predominantly in the south-west. The Isle of Purbeck has a variation of shove-ha'penny which uses a much bigger board marked out with a pattern rather resembling that of an association football pitch.

A full-sized snooker or billiard table is so expensive and takes up so much space that it is rarely seen in pubs today. London is very badly off in this respect. Ten years ago I knew of five or six London pubs with tables: the Baynard Castle, conveniently close to *The Times* and *The Observer*, had about five. Now I know of only one in London, and that is for members only. Seaside towns are better provided for, and when you are lucky enough to find a table that is in good condition and not in use, then there are few prospects more enticing than that great expanse of green.

Bar billiards is much easier to come by, and should not be despised by those who are accomplished on the big table. At first sight it looks as though with a little practice nothing could be easier than endlessly to drop the balls down the 30, 20 and 10 holes at the end of the table. You'll discover there's more to it than that when the local champion arrives on his Suzuki, kicks his crash-helmet under the table and starts putting the balls in the dangerous but valuable 50, 100 and 200 holes, protected as they are by pins (or in some cases wooden mushrooms) which if knocked over lose you the whole break (or in the case of the 200 hole, your entire score).

Bar billiards is played against the clock. After a given period, usually 10 to 15 minutes, your time is up, a bar comes down and the potted balls are no longer returned to you. With the American game of Pool, a welcome new-comer to pub games, the system is different. The many-coloured balls are sunk only once, whereas the white cue-ball continues to be returned to the player. This is made possible by the fact that the white ball is slightly smaller, and thereby able to pass through a throating device which holds back the bigger coloured balls. This has considerable implications for the style of play. Since the cue ball is hitting an object heavier than itself it behaves quite differently from when balls of equal size collide. This requires subtle adjustments to your calculations. Pool is an enjoyable game, though it always seems to be over rather quickly, and to be on the expensive side.

Very old games somehow survive, and even make come-backs. Around Lewes in Sussex you will occasionally find pubs (such as the Lewes Arms, Lewes, a Beard's pub, good beer) which have a very rare game called Toad in the Hole. A box stands on a chair at the side of the room. The box has a drawer in it. The top slopes slightly, is made of lead and has a small hole in the middle. Players take it in turns to throw four heavy metal discs, one at a time, from a distance of eight feet, in the hope that they will go in the hole (being retrieved by opening the drawer). You score two points for a toad in the hole, one if it stays on the lid, and nothing if it skids off and hits the ground. Play is up to 31, ending on an exact score (that is to say, if you need three then you must get three: four busts you, and you have to have another go at three). It's a game of great skill, and is enormously noisy.

Another rarity is Ringing the Bull. A metal ring hangs by a rope from the ceiling, and the aim is to swing the ring across the room to land it on a horn or hook attached to the wall. At Ye Old Trip to Jerusalem in Nottingham it's a real bull's horn, and I'm told that there's a pub in Chiddingstone where the target is an entire stuffed bull's head complete with horns and a ring in its nose.

A brave attempt has been made by Bass Charrington to revive Merels or Nine Men's Morris, though for some inscrutable brewers' reason they have changed its name to Nine Men's Welcome. Shakespeare mentions it as an outdoor game in *A Midsummer Night's Dream* but the design of the board has been found in Viking burial ships and ancient Egyptian roofslabs. As in Noughts and Crosses, the aim is to make a row of three, but there's more to it than that.

A game that needs no equipment and that is usually played near to closing time is Spoof. This is an extremely dangerous game, even though it can be played sitting down. Each player (minimum three, though it's better with four or more) has three coins or other small objects. On the given word each player bangs on the table or bar counter a clenched fist which conceals three coins, two, one or none. The aim is to guess the total number of coins held: no player may guess a number already chosen. Thus, if there are four players, the bidding and thinking might go like this. Smith starts the bidding with 8. Since the possible answer with four players must lie between 12 and 0, this suggests that Smith holds two or three. Jones bids six, which suggests he holds a low number – one or none. Brown bids seven. This leaves the fourth player, Pygge-Strangeways, in a predicament. He cannot go for a middle score, since six, seven and eight have all been pre-empted. He goes for nine. All hands are shown and the total comes to seven. Brown, who called this number, drops out.

The remaining three play another round, which is won by Smith who is eliminated. This leaves the final to Jones and Pygge-Strangeways. Jones wins, and Pygge-Strangeways buys a round.

Spoof is an interesting game of bluff and counter-bluff, calling for psychological insight and low cunning, especially in an established school where players know one another's game. When play is fast, the rounds follow at alarming speed, and when closing time is approaching and Pygge is paying there is a tendency to switch to spirits. This is why Spoof is so dangerous. Full many a glorious morning have I seen turned into a completely wasted afternoon by an injudicious game of Spoof.

In the West country there is a variation of Spoof called Kennoble or Kannoble (something like that). The only difference is that in the last rounds, when there are only two players left, the first player is not allowed to make an impossible call. Thus if he is holding none, it is not possible for the total to be four, five or six.

Skittles is not really a game but a family of games which includes the rare Kent table-game called Daddlums; Table skittles, Bar skittles or Devil-among-the-Tailors, where the ball is swung from the top of a pole, very popular in the Potteries; Alley skittles, to be found in many West country pubs; the splendid London skittles, played in only four places, in which a vast bowl, called a cheese, made of lignum vitae and weighing up to 12 pounds, is hurled at the skittles.

The variation I know best is Aunt Sally, an outdoor game played only around Oxford and Abingdon. It's rather like a cross between skittles and a coconut shy, since instead of throwing a ball at the pins you throw pins at the ball. At the receiving end of the pitch is a screen usually made of green canvas, in front of which stands a post with a swan's neck swivel top on which is balanced a piece of wood painted white and about the size of a jam-jar. This is called the Doll, and the object is to knock the Doll off its perch by throwing sticks underarm from a distance of 30 feet. The sticks look rather like rolling-pins and you have six. Each team has eight players who throw six sticks each, which comprises a round, called a Horse. A match is the best of three horses. The Doll must be knocked off cleanly: it's no good striking the post and toppling it off that way. It is very difficult.

Crown bowls is still popular in the North but under constant threat from the brewers who see bowling greens as potential car parks. The only consolation is that with a little improvisation and a reasonable quantity of fine gravel a car park can make a good pitch for another recent arrival, the French version of bowls, *boules* or *pétanque*.

If the car park is enormous then it can be used for another newcomer. Flinging the Wellington Boot apparently originated in Gerrigong, New South Wales, in 1971. A size 8 man's boot must be used, weighing not more than 37 and not less than 34 ounces, and its shape may not be altered in any way so as to improve its aerodynamics. Distances of over 100 feet have been thrown. I rather despised this bizarre-sounding sport until I had personal experience of it. For some reason it is extremely hard to let go of the boot, which means that some huge contestants throw the boot with great force straight up in the air. More than once I have seen the boot land behind the thrower. Whether welly-flinging will catch on remains to be seen. I rather hope it does.

There are other modern games that are most enjoyable. Table football and pin-tables are excellent in the right pub.

Many video games have been introduced recently. These usually represent a sport such as squash or tennis on a television screen. Players twiddle knobs to intercept the trajectory of the ball, represented by a moving point of light, with symbolic rackets. These games demand quick reactions rather than skill or imagination. They are fun to play once or twice but the novelty wears off, and by the standards of good pub games they are expensive.

Well away from the centre of sanity is dwile flonking. In this game, or possibly sport, a circle of girters dances round a member of the opposing team who revolves in the opposite direction holding a driveller. Sometimes the driveller is called a swadger, and some say that in remote rural areas swadge-copers still survive, selling them as they always have by the tandwainer's nard. The dwile is placed on the end of the driveller. When the accordion stops playing the batsman flonks the dwile at one of the girters, scoring three points for a wanton, two for a marther, and one for a ripple. If he is unlucky enough to swadge then he has to sink a potty before the girters have had time to pass the dwile to the end of the line. Otherwise he loses a point.

In case that is not perfectly clear I'll try again. Two teams, each consisting of twelve idiots, turn up at a pub wearing smocks, boots and old hats. String is tied round the knees to stop rats running up, and a straw is placed in the corner of the mouth. The fielding team join hands, form a circle and prance round a batsman from the other team who holds a cloth soaked in beer slops on the end of a broom handle. When the music stops he flicks this at one of the fielders and scores three if he hits a head, two for a hit on the body and one for a hit on the legs. If after two goes he has failed to score he has to drink six pints of beer from a chamber-pot before the beer-soaked rag has been passed down the line of opponents who are all shouting Pot, Pot, Pot. When all twelve men have had two innings the one with the most points is declared the winner and everyone collapses in a heap until it's time to go back to the asylum.

The players, whom I suspect are defrocked Morris men, will tell you that the game is immensely ancient, and will refer you back to the Waverney rules of 1585. Some people are completely taken in and really believe it to be an immensely ancient game. Timothy Finn's book on pub-games sits on the fence by saying that according to some accounts dwile flonking (or dwyle flunking, as he calls it) was a court pastime of King Offa of Mercia, and according to others was thought up by an underworked BBC man in a long tea-break. On the other hand Arthur Taylor's study of pub games says quite firmly that it was invented by Michael Bentine or his scriptwriters for a sketch in the television programme *It's a Square World* in the late 1960s. Certainly it smacks of Rambling Sid Rumpole, or whatever his name was in *Round the Horne*, and must surely have originated around that time, but it must at least slightly pre-date Mr Bentine's show, as I am assured that it was played at Leeds University in the late 1950s. Its origins appear to be lost in the mists of modernity.

Dwile flonking is not the only game of what Mr Taylor calls total lunacy. In Marrow Dangling human beings are the skittles and vegetable marrows the projectiles. In Rhubarb Thrashing blindfolded and ear-plugged contestants stand on barrels grasping each other's wrists and belabouring one another about the head with sticks of rhubarb. Passing the Splod is a relay race in which the baton is a rubber plunger of the kind used for unblocking sinks: this is attached to the runner's stomach by suction. The difference between Conger Cuddling and Devil-among-the-Tailors is that in Conger Cuddling the skittles are human beings on upturned flower-pots, and the rope and ball is replaced by a conger eel.

Marbles, quoits, bat and trap, knur and spell, drinking games (yards of ale and puzzle mugs), tiddleywinks, conkers, beer-mat flipping and countless other games ancient, modern and improvised, all flourish in publand. Seeking them out and playing them is an inexhaustible, though often exhausting, pursuit.

7 The sound of music

There are pub purists – some would say pub Puritans – who are opposed to any music in any pub. Piped music is certainly a terrible thing, in pubs or anywhere else, and juke boxes have ruined as many good pubs as they emit decibels. Live music is a different matter: the old boy in the village inn who takes out his mouth-organ, gives it a wipe and tries to remember 'Nellie Dean'; the itinerant folk-songsters with their fiddles and accordions and penny whistles; the Saturday night sing-song with the out-of-tune piano and the old dears belting out 'Knees Up Mother Brown', 'Underneath the Arches' and 'Lily of Laguna'; the jazz bands and the rock-and-roll groups: in the right pub at the right moment all have their place. In a pub where there are a lot of young people and a pin-table then even a juke box can be great fun, especially if it still carries golden oldies like 'River Deep and Mountain High', or the Beach-boys' 'Good Vibrations' or Buddy Holly's 'Peggy Sue.' These are special cases. In most pubs at most times music is a menace, since it makes conversation difficult, or even impossible, and because it is usually such horrible music anyway.

8 Signs and wonders

The Romans identified wine-shops by hanging bunches of ivy outside. Mediaeval alehouses were likewise identified by a bush or ale-stake, which was a pole that projected from the front of the building and was decorated with foliage. From these beginnings the inn-sign developed, with the addition of pictures of reigning kings or queens, the heraldry of local grandees, portraits of heroes of the day, or pictures showing the sporting or professional interests of the clientele.

To this day heraldic signs are still frequent. Common ones are the White Hart (Richard II), the Red Lion (John of Gaunt), the Boar's Head (Richard III), the Feathers (Black Prince), the Sun (House of York), the Bear and Ragged Staff (Warwick). In addition there are countless straightforward portraits of kings and queens to represent the Queen's Head and the King's Head. The surprising number of William IV signs testifies not only to pubmen's admiration of this bibulous monarch, but also to the exceptional number of pubs that were built during his reign.

Contemporary heroes have always been represented. When the Elizabethan clown Dick Tarlton was so honoured, Bishop Hall commented in his Satires:

O honour far beyond a brazen shrine
To sit with Tarlton on an ale-post sign.

It accords a strange kind of immortality. Dashingly though the Marquis of Granby behaved at the Battle of Minden in 1759, without the pubs named after him he would be quite forgotten. What the Duke of Cumberland and the Duke of York did to deserve a similar distinction I have no idea. The greatest honour of all is to have a pub named after you in your lifetime. As far as I know the only ones at the time of writing are the Lord Stokes in Leyland; the Charlie Chaplin (the Tarlton of his day) at the Elephant and Castle; the Lord Mancroft at Thorpe St Andrew, near Norwich; the Charlie Butler, a Young's house in Mortlake High Street (for many years Charlie Butler looked after Young's splendid dray-horses); the Giles in Prebend Street, Islington, where the cartoonist was born;

and I've heard that there's a Sir Alf Ramsey in either
Tonbridge or Tunbridge Wells. The Order of the Garter
is limited to 25, the Order of Merit to 24, and the Thistle
admits only 16: at a mere half dozen, having a pub named
after you would appear to be the most exclusive honour of
all.

Pubs called the Mitre are to be found in cathedral towns,
whereas most naval ports have an Anchor or Crown and
Anchor. Many pubs take their names from crafts and
occupations – such as the Wheatsheaf (bakers), the Brick-
layer's Arms, the Woodman, the Shepherd's Rest, the
Saddler's Arms, the Three Compasses (the crest of the
carpenters). Myth is represented by the George and Dragon,
legend by such heroes as the Pindar of Wakefield and the
Miller of Mansfield. The Crusades are remembered in
the Saracen's Head, the Lamb and Flag (the coat of arms
of the Knights Templar) and the Old Trip to Jerusalem.
Changing forms of transport can be traced as the Coach
and Horses gives way to the Railway Tavern. As we have
already seen, there are a great many names to do with
games and sports. Some names are simply odd, like The
Case is Altered, The World Turned Upside Down, The
Who'd Have Thought It? and Orwell's The Moon Under
Water. The shortest pub name appears to be the H.H.
at Cheriton, Hampshire, while the London, Chatham and
Dover Railway Tavern, London SW11, and the Shoulder
of Mutton and Cucumber Inn in Sussex, must be among
contenders for the longest. The Crown, in various combina-
tions (especially with the Rose) is the commonest pub name:
there are about 1,000 examples. Some 900 Red Lions
come in second place.

The inn-sign is one traditional feature of the pub that
the big brewers have not tried to do away with. However,
they increasingly produce signs painted in an impersonal
and lifeless style with an unsympathetically hard finish.
This is the inevitable result of giving the job to the design

department of the company's central office. The signs they produce are the visual equivalent of keg beer. It would be far better to leave the job to local initiative and talent. Doubtless there would be some very crude results, but there would also be far more distinctive, original and witty ones.

Incidentally, pub signs are a good way of keeping children or adults occupied on long car journeys. Various games can be devised. The simplest is for two players to take one side of the road each, scoring one point for every leg seen on an inn-sign. The Cock thus scores two, the White Horse four. The Fox and Hounds is usually accepted as a knock-out victory.

9 Design and development

The most important thing about a pub, more important than the beer itself, is its atmosphere. This is difficult to define but easy to feel. It is made up of many things that have already been considered – the customers, the guvnor, the conversation, the games, the food and drink, the music or lack of it. As important as any of these is the architecture.

The brewers have repeatedly made two major mistakes in pub design. One is to suppose that atmosphere has something to do with oak beams and horse brasses, whereas it is much more a matter of the way the pub's space is divided and subdivided into areas that are public, semi-public, semi-private and private.

A French or Italian café is as open as possible. It is an extension of the street rather than an escape from it. When weather permits the customers actually sit out on the pavement, observing and being observed by passers-by. It is a lay-by for urban pedestrians. By contrast the pub is a secluded place, a warm, cosy haven and refuge from the cares of the world. With its heavy doors, curtains and frosted windows the pub cuts itself off as much as possible from the hustle and bustle of the street. Not only are you hidden from those outside, but a multiplicity of small bars, divisions, screens and partitions enables you to hide from other customers. That strange piece of bar furniture called the snob-screen, which holds a series of pivoted opaque glass windows, can hide you even from the bar-staff (examples in London can be found at The Lamb, Lamb's Conduit Street; Holland's, Exmouth Street, Stepney; and The Bunch of Grapes, Brompton Road, Kensington). Thus developed the usual pub layout. From a central serving area – horseshoe-shaped, oval, semi-circular, or even completely circular – radiates a complex of bars, nooks and snugs with names that vary according to the part of the country – Public Bar, Private Bar, Saloon Bar, Lounge Bar, Ladies' Bar, Bottle and Jug, Four-Ale Bar, Tap-room, Vault, Vaults, Smoke-Room and so on.

These divisions and sub-divisions give the pub its feeling of comfort. It is social comfort rather than physical, and the brewers' second mistake is to suppose that pub comfort is something to do with deep-piled carpets and upholstered chairs. If you feel relaxed and at home you won't mind standing, or sitting on a hard wooden stool or bench. If you feel out of place, you'll be uncomfortable however well-upholstered the seat may be.

To make a huge, but I hope justifiable, generalization, all pubs can be divided into two contrasting kinds which can be given one of two sets of labels – rough or smooth, hard or soft, country or town, village inn or gin-palace, Home from Home or Grander than Home (a distinction made by the authors of *Inside the Pub*). The terms are not precise or always literally exact. There are village inns in the middle of London, for example. There is an overlap and interaction between them, but usually there is not much difficulty in deciding to which of these sets of terms a particular pub belongs. At the same time, though a pub may be mainly hard or mainly soft, if it has both a public bar and a saloon bar it will in some measure contain both.

The pub is a hybrid. On the one side its ancestry can be traced from the drinking-house which provided for a regular local trade: on the other it comes from the rather grander premises where travellers could refresh themselves with food, drink and sleep. Writing about the establishments on the roads to Rome, Horace (Satire 1.5) makes precisely this distinction between the drinking places (*diversoriae*) and the *tabernae*, at which travellers could stay. Whether or not the Romans brought the two types of establishment with them, the Anglo-Saxons had both the alehouse or winehouse for drinking in, and the *cumen-hus* which offered accommodation as well. The distinction continues with the development of the pub or alehouse and the inn or hotel. The family tree therefore looks something like this:

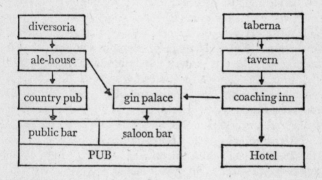

In 1577 Dover harbour was in need of repair and by some bizarre train of thought it was decided that the people to foot the bill should be the publicans of England and Wales, each of whom had to fork out two shillings and sixpence. The census of taverns, inns and alehouses that was taken while collecting this money showed that there were 19,759 licensees in England and Wales. H. A. Monckton calculates that on the basis of a population of 3,700,000 this meant one licence for every 187 of the population, which is about four times as many pubs per head as we have today.

Their quality varied considerably. Doubtless there were many that were as revolting as Elynour Rummyng's establishment. We have already seen that Skelton was not flattering about either her appearance or her brewing methods: her pub and customers were no better. They were of a lewd sort and worse than slovenly in their clothing:

> Some wenches come unlaced,
> Some housewives come unbraced,
> With their naked paps,
> That flips and flaps.

The place is full of swine (the non-human kind);

> The sow with her pigs,
> The bore his tale wriggs,
> His rump also he frigs
> Against the high bench.
> With, Fo, there is a stench.'

An interesting detail is that Elynour not only allowed tick but also permitted customers to pay in kind:

> Instead of coin and money
> Some brought her a conny [rabbit]
> And some a pot with honey . . .
> . . . Some apples, some pears,
> Some brought their clipping-shears,
> Some brought this and that,
> Some brought I wote nere what,
> Some brought their husband's hat,
> Some puddings and links,
> Some tripes that stinks.

This practice is by no means unknown today, when a customer might well exchange a pint for a packet of razor blades that fell off a lorry, or in country districts a hare or pheasant that unfortunately got run over.

Not all pubs were as unsalubrious as Elynour's. In his 1577 *Description of England* Harrison wrote that 'the world

affords not such inns as England has'. London inns were the
worst but even they were better than any abroad. Some of
them were evidently substantial buildings. Harrison speaks
of inns that could lodge and provide meals for as many
as 300. Few of these great coaching inns survive. The Great
Fire destroyed most of those in London, though on the
South bank there still stands The George, Borough High
Street, Southwark, as an example of the splendours of the
great galleried coaching inns. Others survive in many
country towns, complete with paved courtyard and stables
for horses.

Such establishments, for the refreshment and repose of
travellers, were obviously indispensable. The authorities
did not take the same view of the alehouse where the local,
non-travelling drinker unnecessarily and self-indulgently
refreshed himself. An Act of James I, a thoroughly unpleasant man, laid down that the ancient, true and principal
use of winehouses, alehouses and victualling houses was for
the receipt, lodging and relief of wayfaring people and not
for the entertainment and harbouring of lewd and idle
people to waste their time and money in a drunken manner.
Accordingly it was enacted that only travellers could use
such places, while locals were limited to a paltry one hour
at dinner time. These restrictions were not eased until the
Restoration.

In the eighteenth century inns and alehouses alike were
infected with the squalor of the gin epidemic. In his *History
of England*, 1752, Smollett says the suburbs of London
'abounded with an incredible number of public-houses,
which continually resounded with the news of riot and
intemperance. They were the haunts of idleness, fraud and
rapine, and the seminaries of drunkenness, debauchery,
extravagance, and every vice incident to human nature.'
But the pub, then as always, is a split personality, at one
moment plumbing the lower depths of depravity, at the
next aspiring to the loftiest ideals and being acclaimed as the

highest invention of social organization devised by human ingenuity. John Earle described the tavern as 'the busy man's recreation, the idle man's business, the melancholy man's sanctuary, the stranger's welcome, the Inns of Court man's entertainment, the scholar's kindness and the citizen's courtesy.' (*Microcosmographie*, 1628)

This kind of pub, as opposed to the squalid gin-shops, reached a peak of respectability in the late eighteenth century when Dr Johnson testified that 'there is nothing which has yet been contrived by man, by which so much happiness is produced, as by a good tavern or inn.' The country inn won from Goldsmith as fulsome a tribute as Johnson gave the urban one:

> Low lies that house where nut-brown draughts inspired,
> Where grey-beard mirth and smiling toil retired;
> Where village statesmen talked with looks profound,
> And news, much older than the ale, went round.

In design and architecture the eighteenth-century pub was almost indistinguishable from other domestic buildings. Indeed the joke of what is perhaps the funniest play ever written depends on this very point. In Goldsmith's *She Stoops to Conquer* Tony Lumpkin dupes Marlow into believing he is staying at a country inn. In fact he is in the private house of his prospective father-in-law whom he mistakes for the publican, and treats accordingly.

On the other hand the modern town pub complete with inn-sign can begin to be distinguished in some of Hogarth's paintings and engravings, and by the end of the century the pub as we know it was taking shape. Starting in London the brewers became fewer, bigger and stronger and began to take over the retail outlet (or pubs, as they are called). They probably didn't have to try very hard. An easy-going publican asks for credit; this builds up until it is more than he can pay off; soon he has mortgaged the property to the brewery, which gives him easy terms on condition that he does not buy his beer elsewhere. Thus began the tied house system, and with the tied house came the custom-built pub built in a style which spanned the nineteenth century.

10 The gin-palace

From time to time, Dickens wrote in *Sketches by Boz*, 1836, an epidemic breaks out in various trades causing the victims to run stark, staring, raving mad. The symptoms, he said, were an inordinate love of plateglass, gilding and gaslights. Eight years previously there had been a nasty outbreak among the linen-drapers and haberdashers which after a while had abated and died away.

A year or two of comparative tranquillity ensued. Suddenly it burst out again among the chemists; the symptoms were the same, with the addition of a strong desire to stick the royal arms over the shop-door, and a great rage for mahogany, varnish, and expensive floor-cloth. Then the hosiers were infected, and began to pull down their shop-fronts with frantic recklessness. The mania again died away, and the public began to congratulate themselves on its entire disappearance, when it burst forth with ten-fold violence among the publicans . . .

The disease spread with unprecedented speed: 'Onward it has rushed to every part of town, knocking down all the old public-houses, and depositing splendid mansions, stone balustrades, rosewood fittings, immense lamps, and illuminated clocks at the corner of every street.' The gin-palace had arrived.

The first recorded use of the term is only two years earlier than when Dickens was writing, but the style itself had been evolving for some twenty years. It is not true, as is sometimes said, that the gin-palace was the product of Wellington's 1830 Beer Act, but that extraordinary piece of legislation certainly gave it a boost. In a great explosion of pub-building, 30,000 new beer houses opened within a year, almost doubling the previous number of licensed premises. The gin-merchants endeavoured to compete with the beer-sellers by the greater opulence of their premises. By later standards the early gin-palaces look positively demure. Indeed Thompson and Fearon's, Holborn Hill, which was begun in 1829 and is claimed as the first gin-palace, looks restrained by any standards; this is not surprising since it was the work of J. B. Papworth, the architect of Regency Cheltenham. There are other surviving urban pubs of the period that are also dignified, classical and controlled. Joseph May's Trafalgar Tavern, Greenwich, built in 1837, is designed in a delightfully elegant Regency style (unfortunately the interior is now Hollywood fake-Regency of a ghastly kind). The Drapers Arms, Barnsbury Street, Islington, built in the 1840s, is a beautifully balanced classical building. These are exceptions. Nature quickly imitated art, and pub-building soon matched Dickens's exuberant description with riots of pilasters, cornices, balustrades, entablatures, gilded columns, mahogany bars and fitments, polished brass and copper, mosaics, tiles, engraved glass and mirrors, all illuminated and reflected by the magic and mystery of gaslighting.

Although Dickens was writing in the infancy of the gin-palace, his description and analysis of them have not been excelled. He points out that they were numerous and splendid in precise proportion not to the wealth of an area but to its poverty.

> The gin-shops in and near Drury-lane, Holborn, St Giles's, Covent-garden, and Clare-market, are the handsomest in London. There is more filth and squalid misery near those great thoroughfares than in any part of this mighty city.

The profusion of elaborate detail, the lavishness and opulence and indulgence in fantasy, afforded a temporary escape from an everyday life of squalor. Like the cinema architecture of the 1920s and 1930s, like the mediaeval church, the gin-palace was a house of dreams where the most wretched could go for an hour or two to escape into a world of fantasy, romance and the illusion of wealth.

As with the church and the cinema, no expense was spared on the gin-palace. As the nineteenth century proceeded, new materials and techniques were enlisted to render them yet more lavish. Massive buildings were erected with equally massive confidence on prominent corner sites. One example is the Salisbury, Green Lanes, Harringey (an area particularly rich in gin-palace survivals). Another is the Archway Tavern, Highgate (1886), which had huge signs proclaiming the name of the pub, proprietor, brewer and beer in defiance of all temperance movements: 'The Archway Tavern, Wheeler & Son, Watney & Company's Fine Ales, Porter, Imperial Stout' (by this time the gin-palaces were selling beer as well as spirits).

The imposing exteriors of the gin-palaces only hinted at the wealth within – mahogany bars and furnishings, wrought iron, mosaic floors, painted tile walls, relief panels of copper and bronze, graining, marbling, lettering, embossed Lincrusta and Anaglypta ceiling-papers almost indistinguishable from moulded plaster-work. Glass was everywhere: stained glass, engraved glass windows, screens, doors and mirrors decorated by the new techniques of brilliant-cutting and acid-etching with intricate designs of foliage, abstract arabesques and fishtailed lettering.

If the gin-palace was a house of dreams, the house of dreams was also a palace of gin. It was a place to get drunk in, and Victorian drinking was very dreadful. In 1900 deaths from alcoholism were 100 per million. During the Second World War they were less than three, rising to five in the mid-1960s. A hundred years ago the consumption of spirits per head was nearly twice what it is now, and in 1875 per capita consumption of beer was 280 pints as against just over 200 pints today. These figures conceal the real situation, since drinking is much more evenly distributed through the population now, and for another thing spirits and beer were very much stronger a century ago than they are today. It was therefore understandable that by the beginning of this century the urban pub had become thoroughly unrespectable. There were always pipe-puffing essayists and tweedy poets to extol the oak beams and ingle-nooks of the rural inn, but the gin-palace was in disgrace.

Victorian churches, domestic buildings, railway stations, and factories are rightly admired and protected. Victorian pubs, more splendid than any of them, have largely been ignored by students and amateurs of architecture. The town guides never fail to direct your attention to some immensely gloomy Victorian church, but it is unlikely that it will direct you to the most splendid of pubs. Professor Pevsner's massive survey of the buildings of England neglects them shamefully. Until quite recently very little was written about them. Gorham and Dunnett's excellent *Inside the Pub* is a quarter of a century old, and there's a thoughtful essay by John Piper. Not until 1975 was there a serious study of them – by Mark Girouard – but even this is virtually restricted to London.

The lack of interest in Victorian pubs enabled the brewers, especially in the 1930s and 1960s, to inflict on them, with scarcely any public protest at all, vandalism that is paralleled in this country only by that visited on ecclesiastical buildings first by Henry VIII and then by Cromwell's soldiery. Dickens wrote about the inordinate love of glass and mahogany as a disease. Ten to fifteen years ago the brewers were seized by the exactly opposite kind of illness and dementedly ripped out mahogany fittings, irreplaceable windows and mirrors and smashed them with hammers. This is not hyperbole. I have seen it done, as anyone with his eyes open must have in the London of the 1960s.

Fragments survived, and nowadays the brewers, themselves dismayed at their own behaviour, are more likely to be buying them back at silly prices from stalls in the Portobello Road to put them into fake Victorian pubs.

The brewers still try to remove pub partitions whenever they are given a chance, and continue their war of attrition against the public bar. They are less given than previously to replacing natural materials with man-made ones (a process described by a friend of mine as formication). A few years ago the big brewers all tried to impose what was called a 'corporate image' on their pubs. This meant that irrespective of historical period or style the pub would be painted in a particular colour scheme. Allied Breweries have uglified many buildings with yellow and brown fascias and an unusually unattractive nonce lettering. Watney's painted their pubs red with the name of the house in letters of white expanded Clarendon bold. This is quite an attractive type. Unfortunately they made it three-dimensional and used a moulded synthetic material, with the result that the letters look like blocks of slightly melted ice-cream. Bass Charrington also splashed the red paint around and put silly illuminated boxes over the doors.

From time to time the brewers still commit atrocities against urban pubs, but they seem to have calmed down a little in the past few years. Now the danger comes mostly from town planners, traffic engineers and property developers who like nothing better than knocking down buildings of character and replacing them with wider roads and lifeless glass-and-concrete filing cabinets. In Manchester, for example, the City Fathers have long held the view that one brick should not be allowed to stand on top of another for more than thirty years. Consequently large areas of the city resemble Dresden in its immediate post-Harris period. The Victorian pubs have been swept away with everything else. Most pubs of merit that have not been destroyed are due to be. One survivor is the Crown and

Kettle (corner of Oldham Street and Great Ancoats Street) which has an enormous, elaborate green-and-cream plaster ceiling, and some fine stained-glass windows which the brewery architect was only prevented from removing by the vigorous protests and petitions of regulars from the neighbouring *Express* building.

Birmingham has also been wanton in its self-destruction. Many fine Victorian pubs have gone, and more are under imminent threat. One that is fortunately safe (though only after a struggle) is the magnificent Barton's Arms in Aston. In an area of total devastation it alone has been allowed to stand, presumably through some aberration or carelessness on the part of the property developers, traffic engineers and city planners, who have doubtless since been reprimanded. Not only has it survived but the brewers, Mitchells and Butlers, have restored it to its former glory. Erected in 1901, it is an ornate red-brick building with an exterior that is impressive enough, but nothing to what you find inside. From the mosaic floor of the entrance to the carved wood round the bar, the elaborate brass gas-fittings, the snob-screen, the cast-iron staircase and the stained-glass windows, the profusion of detail is astounding. Best of all are the tiles that cover every available walled surface, many elaborately modelled in relief, all dazzlingly coloured in reds and blues and greens as brilliant as a newly-opened box of paints. Fine tile-work is a characteristic of pubs in the Birmingham conurbation (the Waterloo Hotel, Smethwick, is another notable example) but the Barton's Arms is the best. If there is a Chartres of tile-work, this must surely be it.

Liverpool still has some magnificent pubs in the gin-palace style. The Vines in Lime Street, an establishment much favoured by cauliflower-eared pugilists, is very fine, with some particulary notable carved wooden caryatids. Even better – indeed, in the Barton's Arms class – is the Philharmonic Hotel, Hope Street, placed conveniently half-way between the Roman Catholic cathedral and the Church of England one. The exterior is what Sir Osbert Lancaster calls Pont Street Dutch, with stepped gables, turrets, bow-windows and wrought-iron gates. Fine though the exterior is, it is again the interior that most amazes and delights, with a dazzling array of mosaics, stained glass, copper friezes, mahogany, tiles and engraved mirrors. The stained-glass windows depict ferociously-moustached men who look like Kitchener, Roberts and Baden-Powell and probably are. Some are less military; in tribute to the nearby concert hall one announces that Music is the Universal Language of Mankind. Even the Gents is magnificent. Everything in it is marble except for the taps of gleaming brass, the coloured tiles, the Adamant cistern and the lead-less-glazed ceramic work which is the creation of Twyfords Ltd. There are many contenders for the title of worst pub lavatory; this one has no rival claimant to that of best.

Dublin and Belfast both used to have many magnificent nineteenth century pubs. Dublin's have been badly depleted by property developers, Belfast's savagely by bombs.

London has far more surviving gin-palaces than any other city, though none that is to my mind quite as impressive as the Barton's Arms or the Philharmonic. The Red Lion, Duke of York Street, off St James's Square, is usually so crowded as to reproduce accurately the conditions of the London undergound in the rush-hour. If you can, visit it at an off-peak moment it reveals itself to be a tiny jewel of a pub, brilliant with engraved, cut and etched glass. The Bunch of Grapes, 207 Brompton Road, is notable for its ornate wood-carving, mirrors, snob-screens and many divisions. The three small bars and the large saloon bar are partitioned from one another, but inter-connected by small doorways, thereby creating the complex spatial arrangement and pub atmosphere discussed earlier.

The Salisbury in St Martin's Lane has a classic Victorian interior of mahogany, cut glass and red velvet upholstery with large art nouveau copper lampstands in the form of bare-breasted Dianas and hounds. The Viaduct Tavern, 126 Newgate Street, has suffered at various times from the attention of the brewers and from bombs at the nearby Old Bailey. It is still worth visiting for the carved wooden screens, with finely engraved glass panels, some pleasant nineteenth-century paintings (one with a bullet hole in it, fired by a drunken soldier during the war), and Lincrusta ceiling. Not far away at 209 High Holborn is my favourite Watney's pub, the Princess Louise, with marble pillars and a large bay window dominating the exterior: inside are the most lovely walls on which multicoloured floral tiles alternate with cut-glass mirrors.

Those mentioned so far are in areas much frequented by visitors to London. Some of the best gin-palaces in London are off the beaten tourist track in Harringey. The original customers must have been people like Lupin Pooter, the alarmingly modern son in *The Diary of a Nobody*. As the underground railway network expanded, the Pooters and other commuting City workers moved out also. Harringey declined, which was the saving of the great pubs. The area became so depressed that the brewers didn't think the pubs worth spending money on. They consequently suffered from neglect but not from the tarting-up or outright destruction that ruined so many pubs in more affluent areas such as Chelsea. In the nineteenth-century pubs of Harringey the mirrors may be cracked, the brass tarnished, the paintwork grimy. Dapper Lupin Pooter has been replaced by West Indians and Irish labourers, and the tipple is not gin but Guinness. But apart from these superficial changes the pubs of Harringey have survived much better than in most areas. Particularly notable are the Beaconsfield, the Queen's and – best of all – the Salisbury, with its superb iron, glass and mosaic and a magnificent turret jutting from the corner of the building supported by a single granite column.

I have left till last a London pub which is so eccentric that it does not properly belong to the gin-palace tradition or, indeed, to any other. The Black Friar, 174 Queen Victoria Street, EC4, is *sui generis*, a one-off job never to be repeated. This wedge-shaped building stuck under Blackfriars railway bridge has fortunately survived the development that has devastated most of the area. It was built in 1903, designed by H. Fuller Clark with embellishments by the sculptor Henry Poole R.A., as he signs his work all over the building. The pub stands on the site of a former thirteenth century Dominican priory, and the exterior is decorated with mosaics, statues and relief carvings depicting scenes of monastic life. There are monks fishing, eating and laughing. On the corner, smiling across the Thames, is a huge statue of a fat, jolly Friar Tuck figure. The pub's interior is even more remarkable, with its embellishments of polished stone, marble and alabaster, a massive open fire with ingle-nooks, and more mosaics and reliefs depicting friars fishing and drinking. At the back an enchanting small room contains further mosaics, medallions and bronze inscriptions bearing such mottoes as 'A good thing is soon snatched away', 'Don't advertise, tell a gossip', 'Haste is slow' and the inscrutably enigmatic 'Tomorrow is Friday'.

11 The country pub and the public bar

The gin-palace was a product of the nineteenth century, developed by identifiable architects and builders. By contrast the village inn, and the public bar style, are traditional forms of much greater antiquity. The eighteenth-century alehouse, such as Tony Lumpkin's haunt, the Three Jolly Pigeons, would have been furnished much like the living-room or kitchen of any other house in the village. In country areas there are still to be found pubs that don't even have a bar. Instead the beer is carried through on a tray from the kitchen or up from the cellar. With their wooden beams, flagstones or brick floors, their scrubbed wooden tables, their high-backed settles and church-pew benches polished by generations of elbows and bottoms, these pubs have changed hardly at all since Morland depicted them in the eighteenth century. I know one such on the Norfolk Broads that hasn't even electricity.

The first cautious evolutionary step would have been a serving-hatch from the kitchen, or else a half-door with a ledge on top, to rest drinks and exchange money on. With this rudimentary bar-counter the room now had two focal points, the other being the open fireplace. For normal purposes this was sufficient, but if the squire looked in with the doctor or his estate manager, then the landlord might show these distinguished people into his private sitting-room. This would be the equivalent to the front parlour in a working-class home, spotlessly clean and tidy and hardly ever used. As opposed to the sternly functional furnishings of the public bar or tap room, the values here in the lounge or saloon are would-be genteel with heavy drapery, antimacassars and kitsch objects.

The lounge, or saloon, always tends towards ostentation, with its purples and crimsons, concealed lighting, plastic flowers and landlord's bric-à-brac and souvenirs of Mediterranean holidays. The public bar remains uncompromisingly unassuming, with the austerity, control and simplicity usually associated with Japanese design. Nothing is exaggerated, and only natural materials are used. By way of decoration there may be a twelve-year-old photograph of the Queen on a horse, or perhaps a pin-up calendar advertising the local coal-merchant's wares. Otherwise little more than a few well-worn kitchen chairs, a table for playing dominoes, a dart-board, a notice-board with the cricket or football fixtures, an open fire, ash-trays and (ideally) a Guinness toucan lamp.

The dado (the lower part of an interior wall) is usually

in tongue-and-groove matchboarding of irregular width, finished at the top with a simple rounded moulding. The wood is either left plain or else painted with an undercoat and then given a simulated grain (scumbled, brush- or comb-grained) and finally varnished. The upper part of the wall and the ceiling will be cream, but subtly browned by the rising nicotine of countless smoky evenings. The classic scheme of the public bar thus ranges from pale yellow to all the various shades of dark brown – chestnut brown, mouse brown, chocolate brown, toffee brown. The public bar is, in Lewis Mumford's vivid phrase, a symphony in brown. The colours are those of wood, from pale pine to rich dark mahogany. They are also, as Ben Davis has pointed out, the colours of beer, from light ale to stout. By contrast the saloon bar colours are those of saloon bar drinks, from wine reds to the shrill green of crème de menthe and even the blue of Bols Curaçao.

The vocabulary of the public bar tradition is made up of many tiny details, from the shape of the mouldings to the profile of bench ends. Even in towns it still carries a reminder of the old country kitchen. It is one of the few examples of architectural popular art. The idea of popular art is familiar in music, painting and even literature, but has been ignored in architecture. The traditional public bar or country inn is an art form of the people, and a vernacular one. It is subtle and rich, and the tradition is still alive, though under constant attack from the brewers.

The Erroll Report noted in 1972 a 'discernible trend towards the abolition of the public bar and its replacement by one-bar public houses offering relatively luxurious long-bar type facilities . . .' On the face of it the abolition of the public bar might look soundly democratic, and it is perfectly true that there are pubs in which the public bar is very depressing. But the public bar is more than an anachronistic survivor from a class-ridden age. For one thing prices are usually lower in the public bar, and it is there that the

games are played. Far from being socially divisive, the
public bar extends the range of class, income and occupa-
tion of those using the pub. Take, for example, the East
India Arms, Fenchurch Street. This is the only Young's
pub in the City of London, and consequently it is very
crowded. It has only one bar. There used to be a notice,
and as far as I know there still is, regretting that customers
in dirty clothing cannot be served. This is understandable,
since most of the customers are City gentlemen, brokers in
foreign exchange, commodities and the like. These men in
100-guinea suits prefer to be jostled by other 100-guinea
suits rather than by men in overalls covered with dust and
plaster from nearby building sites; but a better solution
than a clothing bar would be a public bar. (Incidentally,
this pub has also not got a ladies' lavatory.) In a less extreme
form the same thing is happening in pubs all over the country.
Men who used to drop in for a quick one on their way home
in their working clothes, now have to go home first and
dress up.

Another argument in favour of the public bar: suppose
you like the Red Lion but can't stand Jones who appears
to live there and is a crashing bore; or it may be those
unspeakable copywriters who all laugh too loud; or Smith
who smells and cadges drinks; or Pygge-Strangeways. If
the Red Lion has two bars it is easy to avoid the group or
individual you especially abhor. If it has only one then you
have to find another pub. From this point of view it does
not much matter what the bars look like or what they are
called – public, private, saloon, lounge, vault, tap-room or
even Ye Old Nelle Gwynne Cock-Tayle Barre. The important thing is that the place should be divided up, and that
separate bars should be sub-divided, whether with partitions, screens, benches or tables.

The brewers have been spending some £50 million a
year on 'refurbishing' pubs and building new ones. As a
result pubs are generally far more cheerful than they used

to be. Sometimes the Gents even has a handbasin and running water.

Such changes are welcome. What is not welcome is when some quiet, decent, ordinary pub is closed down and given the treatment. After a few months it reopens in the form of a Wild West saloon, a German bierkeller, an Alpine chalet, a Chinese junk or some such flummery. Some of these defy parody. The *Gloucester Citizen* in December 1974 carried a story headlined 'Pub Plan Raised a Laugh'. The plan was to turn a Whitbread's pub called the Double Gloucester into a medieval castle. Mr David Evans, principal planning assistant, told a council committee that the man who brought the plan in asked for his immediate reaction. 'When I stopped laughing,' said Mr Evans, 'I told him I really didn't know. I said rather than him go to the trouble of preparing detailed drawings, I would find out the committee's view.' Councillor John Robins's reaction was, 'Thank God I live in Hucclecote.' He said the proposed treatment was completely out of character with all the houses along the road.

That one got away. Others were less fortunate. The *Holylake News and Advertiser* (August 1974) carried a report rich in irony, though whether intentional or not I am unable to decide:

West Kirby's oldest pub, the Ring o' Bells, reopens on Friday after extensive alterations transforming the popular public house into an olde worlde taverne. Equipped with fibre-glass imitation wooden beams jutting low, subtle, thick carpets and comfortable seats the pub has been altered beyond all recognition. Gone is the lounge with partitions separating three enclaves. There's a fire, too, consisting of lava rocks to give the impression of a real fire. Applications are in to increase the car parking facilities on the surrounding land which is owned by Whitbread's.

A death sentence for the bowling green, no doubt.

An outrageous case of which I have personal knowledge is the White Horse, Bearsted, near Maidstone, Kent. Bearsted has an enormous village green where W. G. Grace played cricket. It is surrounded by chestnut trees, half-timbered and Georgian houses, and you can glimpse the church and some oast houses in the distance. The village scene is completed by the shop and the pub. When I went there in September 1973 the public bar had old high-backed chairs, dark wooden beams, rows of pewter mugs and a dart-board. There was real beer for 13p a pint (15p in the saloon bar). On the counter was a plump vegetable marrow, the subject of a competition that was in progress. On payment of 5p you wrote down your name and estimate of the marrow's weight. The competition would be closed when enough had been raised to pay for a bottle of whisky, to be awarded to whoever guessed closest.

There was another list of names in circulation: a petition to the brewery not to modernize the pub. 'Why don't they modernize Stonehenge? Why don't they modernize Westminster Abbey?' a New Zealander demanded savagely, as he added his name to the list. He was on a nostalgia trip, having been stationed in Bearsted in the war.

Work had already started on the rambling buildings at the back of the pub, which were in a very poor state of repair. It was the pub itself that customers were worried about. They spoke of such coming horrors as plastic beams (in a building full of real oak ones) and said they had seen plans showing the pub with only one bar. This would mean the disappearance of the public bar and the dart-board.

I took this up with Whitbread's, who assured me that it was all a false alarm and the villagers were mistaken. They said the work would be confined to the building in the rear that was being made into a restaurant. The pub itself would not be touched other than to replace some rotten floorboards. I was glad to receive Whitbread's word that there were no plans to remove the public bar.

In April 1974 I received a letter from someone who said the White Horse had reopened, that the changes were considerable and execrable, and that the public bar and dart-board had gone. Whitbread's confirmed that such was the case. They said they had discovered that the foundations were rotten and they had had to do more work than anticipated. They did not explain why the new foundations could not support a public bar or a dart-board.

When I visited the new White Horse a few months later I was expecting (perhaps even intending) to dislike what they had done. This turned out to be more difficult than I had expected. It is true that there were thick carpets everywhere, concealed lighting and the inescapable piped music. It is true that the real beer had been replaced by top-pressure at 18p in the Yeoman's Bar and 20p in the Cocktail Bar. It is also true that the public bar and the dart-board had gone, and that the whole place had been done up in the vilest of brewers' taste (and taste doesn't come any viler than that). But it was so utterly, completely bogus that it had a distinct quality of the 1960s' camp kind that should appeal to amateurs of kitsch.

Connoisseurs of anachronism too. Anyone who has enjoyed spotting slaves wearing wristwatches in a Cecil B. de Mille biblical epic would enjoy this place. The *Morning Advertiser* captured the spirit with hilarious, if not intentional, accuracy:

> Facing the village green, the White Horse was a pleasant but unremarkable sixteenth-century inn to which in Victorian times a large hall or club room had been added . . . In the conversion the atmosphere of the medieval inn has been enhanced; two original fireplaces, probably early Stuart, were discovered and have been exposed . . . The 'T'-shaped club room, now named 'Camelot Hall' has been transformed into a baronial dining hall.

The brewer's designers, like the *Morning Advertiser* reporter, happily equate the Middle Ages (say AD 1000 to 1500) not only with the sixteenth century, the Stuarts (seventeenth century) and Victorian times (c. 1840–1900) but also with the Arthurian period, an error of about half a millenium in the other direction.

This delicious jumble is tricked out with such refinements as machine-sawn beams with fake adze marks (an increasingly popular kitsch cliché), heraldic banners, fibre-glass battle-axes, crossed swords and armour, plastic gauntlets, fibre-glass horn lamps, a fibre-glass ball-and-chain, an electric fake-log fire and a low beam on which is written 'Prithee Lower Thy Head'.

In the restaurant the Arthurian theme – incidentally this part of the country is freer of Arthurian associations than most – is suggested by a sword in a stone, and outside the Gents there is a fountain and pool from which emerges a sword-waving arm. It is not clothed in white samite, mystic, wonderful but appears to be that of the man who used to beat the gong in J. Arthur Rank films. As you would expect, it is made of fibre-glass. The whole thing is a hoot.

At the same time that they were thus demolishing a traditional Kentish village pub, Whitbread's were putting up fake Kentish village pubs in France, designed for them by the very firm which perpetrated this nonsense at Bearsted.

To be fair, the new pub has many good points. The Gents is of exemplary cleanliness. Trade seemed to have increased considerably and people to be enjoying themselves. The manager and his wife were pleasant, and assured me that customers did include locals, some of whom had opposed the changes but now welcomed them. On the other hand it had been created at the expense of a very pleasant and unpretentious pub of a kind that exists nowhere else in the world and that is becoming increasingly rare in this country.

What is the essential quality that differentiates the old

White Horse from the new, or any good pub from any indifferent one? In the end, it is not the difference between an oak beam and a fibre-glass one. It's the difference between a place which is the social focus for a community, and one that is merely a commercial enterprise. It's the difference between a pub where for no financial gain someone organizes a competition to guess the weight of a vegetable marrow, and one where it is inconceivable that such a thing could happen. A pub is not just a place for buying and selling food and drink. It is the social and convivial centre of a community. This is why the closing of its only pub can kill a village and turn it into an unorganic huddle of dwellings. After all that has been written in the previous pages about the importance of the beer, the guvnor, the customers, the food, the games and the architecture, I would say that more important than any of them is whether or not a pub can pass the vegetable marrow test.

VII What's Where: A Pubman's Gazetteer

In the following guide to the beer and breweries of the British Isles the words 'real beer' are used to mean traditionally-brewed, unfiltered, naturally-conditioned, living beer. For explanations of other terms see Chapter 3. The face of British brewing is changing rapidly. This account was brought as up-to-date as possible in November, 1976.

England

NORTH (CUMBRIA, NORTHUMBERLAND, DURHAM)

The North-east is rather badly off for real beer. The pubs are dominated by Scottish and Newcastle Breweries, which nowadays serve little that is not pressurized. However, no visit to Newcastle is complete without sampling – even in their present form – S and N's Exhibition (generally known as Ex) and of course Newcastle Brown (pronounced 'broon'). Choice is rather better in Cumberland and Westmorland. The area is the home of the following independent companies:

J. W. Cameron, Lion Brewery, Hartlepool, Co. Durham
Cameron's pubs are the best bet for real beer in the North-east. There are about 700 of them, mostly serving beer by hand or electric pumps. They brew a dark mild, and two bitters, of which the Strongarm is highly esteemed.

Hartley's (Ulverston) Ltd, Old Brewery, Ulverston, Cumbria
Some sixty pubs in the Furness peninsula and Lake District, where many Whitbread pubs also sell Hartley's

beer. The brewery produces only draught beer, Whitbread supplying the bottled. There are two excellent bitters and a dark mild, all served by hand or electric pumps in all their pubs.

Jennings Brothers Ltd, The Castle Brewery, Cockermouth, Cumbria
Some ninety tied houses in western Cumberland, serving excellent bitter and dark mild without top pressure.

Northern Clubs' Federation Brewery, Forth Street, Newcastle upon Tyne
The beer is sold in some 900 clubs in the north of England, and a few in the Midlands, in Cornwall and in the House of Commons. This was the first brewery to declare the original gravities of its beers. The Pale and Special ales are sold in tank and keg form, but to my taste suffer not so much from this as from being sold at sub-Arctic temperatures.

After the First World War working men's clubs had good reason to be dissatisfied with the way in which beer was supplied to them. When beer was scarce the brewers gave priority to their own pubs, and at the same time they kept reducing the strength of the beer while keeping up the prices: in effect they were, as the song has it, the very fat men who water the worker's beer. For the clubs the obvious solution was to brew their own beer, which accordingly they did. Federations of working men's clubs started breweries all over the country. Many of them were still operating fairly recently, but the past twenty years have seen the closure of, among others, the Metropolitan and Home Counties Clubs' Brewery, the Lancashire Clubs' Brewery, the Walsall and District Clubs' Brewery, the Midland Clubs' Brewery and most recently the Yorkshire Clubs' Brewery. The only survivors are the South Wales and Monmouthshire United Clubs' Brewery at Pontyclun, and the Northern Clubs' Federation Brewery in Newcastle upon Tyne. The 'Fed' was founded in 1919, and started

brewing in March 1921. By the next year it was twice
able to cut the price of its beer and to force the other
brewers to do likewise. Since then it has not only survived
but also, through a combination of good beer and good
organization, become exceedingly prosperous.

The clubs and the brewery are mutually dependent.
Usually a brewery owns its retail outlets: here it is the
other way round. The clubs started the brewery, and in
return the brewery paid back to the clubs £20 million in
its first fifty years. It is probably the most successful exercise
in co-operation since the days of the Rochdale pioneers.

Vaux Breweries Ltd, Sunderland
About 600 pubs throughout the North, especially the
North-east. The draught beers are Samson bitter, Lorimer
Best Scotch, Pale Ale and a light mild: unfortunately they
are mostly dispensed by top-pressure from tanks except
along the Tyne valley and around Berwick-upon-Tweed.

Workington Brewery, Workington, Cumbria
After a spell in the hands of Maxwell Joseph's Mount
Charlotte Investments, this brewery was sold to Matthew
Brown of Blackburn in June 1975. 110 pubs in Cumberland
and north Lancashire. The draught bitter and the mild
are both now filtered and pressurized.

NORTH-WEST (LANCASHIRE, CHESHIRE)

An area with an exceptionally wide choice of real beer.
Macclesfield, for example, with a population of 50,000,
has 80 pubs, more than 60 of which serve real beer from
nine different brewers. About three-quarters of the pubs
in Manchester serve real beer. In Rochdale you can choose
from the products of no less than 13 different breweries,
and there are many other towns in Lancashire and Cheshire
that are nearly as well supplied.

The main national companies in the area are Tetley's (Allied) whose beer can be good but is mostly pressurized now, and Wilson's (Watney's) which brews the excellent Great Northern Bitter, unpressurized in more than half of their pubs around Manchester. The independent breweries in the area are:

Boddingtons', Strangeways Brewery, Manchester, Lancashire
About 280 tied houses throughout Lancashire. The draught bitter is very good, and there are also two dark milds and a strong Old. The company's commitment to traditional methods, has won it an enthusiastic following of the kind that Young's of Wandsworth commands in London. In 1970 the company pulled off a magnificent David-and-Goliath act by fighting off a takeover bid by Allied Breweries. Against all expert advice they appealed to shareholders and drinkers to stand up for independent brewing, and subsequent events have magnificently justified their stand, with greatly increased sales and profits.

Matthew Brown, Lion Brewery, Blackburn, Lancashire
More than 600 pubs in north Lancashire and Cumberland. There's a draught bitter and a mild. The company appears to be reversing its earlier policy of going over to top-pressure.

Burtonwood (Forshaws) Ltd, Bold Lane, Burtonwood, Warrington, Cheshire
More than 300 tied houses in central Lancashire, Cheshire, Staffordshire, and North Wales, most of which use hand or electric pumps to serve the pleasant draught bitter and two milds. Bottled beers include four pale ales and a strong dark ale.

Greenall Whitley, Warrington, Cheshire
The largest of all the independent brewing companies with 1,500 tied houses in southern Lancashire, Cheshire, Shropshire and North Wales. The draught bitter, light mild and dark mild are mostly served by pumps without top-pressure.

Higson's, Stanhope Street, Liverpool, Lancashire
About 160 tied houses, mostly on Merseyside, but with several in north Wales. Draught bitter and dark mild are both well thought of and are usually served by traditional methods.

Joseph Holt Ltd, Derby Brewery, Cheetham, Manchester
Some 80 tied houses in the Manchester area. The draught bitter and the dark mild are served by hand or electric pumps in all the pubs.

Hydes' Anvil Brewery, Manchester, Moss Lane West, Manchester
Fifty tied houses in south Manchester and between Chester and Wrexham. Another staunchly traditional brewery. The draught bitter, two milds and strong Anvil ale are all excellent, and served without top-pressure in all the pubs.

J. W. Lees, Greengate Brewery, Middleton Junction, Manchester
Some 200 pubs in Lancashire and Cheshire, mostly around Middleton, Rochdale and Oldham, with about 35 in North Wales. 'John Willie' is very popular and deservedly so. The draught bitter, light mild and dark mild are served without top-pressure in all their pubs. There is a new and powerful draught barley wine called Moonraker.

Mitchells of Lancaster, Moor Lane, Lancaster
Forty-seven tied houses, within ten miles of Lancaster, and three in Yorkshire at Bentham. Two bitters and a dark mild, all invariably served by approved methods.

Oldham Brewery, Albion Brewery, Coldhurst Street, Oldham, Lancashire
About 100 pubs within ten miles of Oldham. The draught bitter and the dark mild are both good, though often sold with top-pressure.

David Pollard, Reddish Vale Industrial Estate, Stockport
Not the biggest, but one of the newest breweries in the country, started by David Pollard in 1975, and developing fast. Pollard's Best Bitter has already won a good reputa-

tion, and amongst other places it is available at the White
Gates, Manchester Road, Hyde, which is one of the five
pubs acquired by Camra's offshoot investment company.

Frederic Robinson, Unicorn Brewery, Stockport, Cheshire
About 300 pubs, mainly in North-east Cheshire and
Manchester, Derbyshire and north Wales. Two bitters,
two delicious light milds almost always sold without top-
pressure, and a draught barley wine called Old Tom which
is very hard to find but very well worth the search – one of
the great beers.

Daniel Thwaites, Star Brewery, Blackburn, Lancashire.
Three hundred and eighty pubs throughout Lancashire,
into Cheshire and down to the Potteries. Thwaites are
proudly traditional, using shire horses to deliver beer in
Blackburn, and at present converting back from tank to
cask beer in the few pubs where the beer was pressurized.
They brew a very pleasant bitter and two milds.

Yates and Jackson, Lancaster, Lancashire
Forty-three tied houses within 25 miles of Lancaster.
Excellent bitter and a pleasant mild, invariably served
without top-pressure.

YORKSHIRE

Yorkshire people, chauvinists about beer as about everything
else, believe they have the best beer in the country. A lot of
it is certainly very good, and doubtless the drinkers' keen
interest in the product keeps the brewers up to scratch. It
is not mere chance that it is in Yorkshire and Lancashire
that Watney's have refrained from messing up the real
beer of Wilson's and Webster's, and Tetley's (Allied)
tastes much more like beer than Allied's Ind Coope does
in the south. Stone's (Bass Charrington) has a strong
following in Sheffield, but Whitbread's Sheffield brewery
(formerly Tennant's) produces no traditional beer, and

Courage's have closed the once-famous Barnsley brewery
and killed off John Smith's in its traditional form.

As with Lancashire, southern visitors to Yorkshire may
get the false impression that all the beer is top-pressure as a
result of confusing keg taps with the bar mountings of the
perfectly acceptable and very widespread electric pumps.
For some reason Yorkshire people consider it very effemi-
nate to drink from a glass with a handle. They also like
the beer to have a big head, and for the foam to stick to
the side of the glass as it goes down.

Yorkshire has the following independent brewing
companies:

W. M. Darley Ltd, Thorne, Doncaster, Yorkshire
More than 100 pubs in an area bounded by Pontefract,
Doncaster, Beverley and Hull, and over to Scunthorpe
and Cleethorpes in Lincolnshire. The draught bitter and
dark mild are mostly on hand or electric pumps.

Hull Brewery, Hull, Yorkshire
Two hundred pubs, nearly half in Hull. The draught bitter,
light mild and dark mild are all filtered, though often served
by traditional means. Since being taken over by Northern
Dairies and being renamed North Country Breweries,
however, the company seems to be turning away from
traditional beer in favour of pressurization and keg beer.
It will be sad if this turns out to be the case.

Selby (Middlesbrough) Brewery, Selby, Yorkshire
Having ceased brewing for eighteen years this company
started up again in 1972. The beer is brewed from malt
and hops without sugar, and is racked into wooden casks.
They have recently reintroduced a Nut Brown Ale and a Pale
Ale brewed to pre-Second World War recipes. The only
tied house is the Board Inn, Howden, south of York, but
the beer is also available in some clubs and free houses
around Selby and York.

Samuel Smith, Old Brewery, Tadcaster, Yorkshire
Nearly 300 tied houses scattered over an area from Tyne-

side to Northamptonshire, concentrated in Yorkshire; also in Rochdale, Oldham and the Manchester area of Lancashire, and recently available in free trade in London. Draught bitter and mild dispensed by hand or electric pumps in most houses.

Timothy Taylor and Co Ltd, Keighley, Yorkshire

Nearly 30 tied houses in Keighley and nearby. Two draught bitters, a dark mild and an old served by hand or electric pump. There is also a strong draught bitter called Draught Landlord which appears to be available only at the Hare and Hounds, Hebden Bridge. Timothy Taylor's pubs are some of the pleasantest in the north of England.

T. and R. Theakston, The Brewery, Masham, Ripon, Yorkshire

Only 8 tied houses in Masham, Ripon and other parts of north Yorkshire, but the company's excellent beer is also widely available in the free trade. The draught bitter is a pale yellow, and its taste arouses controversy between its admirers and detractors. Also on draught are mild and the celebrated strong dark ale called Old Peculier, named after a local ecclesiastical court called the Peculier court. All Theakston's houses use hand or electric pumps.

S. H. Ward and Co. Ltd, Sheaf Brewery, Eccleshall Road, Sheffield

A subsidiary of Vaux with about 100 pubs, mostly in Sheffield. Two draught bitters and a draught mild, mostly served by electric or hand pumps.

WEST MIDLANDS (SHROPSHIRE, STAFFORDSHIRE, HEREFORDSHIRE, WORCESTERSHIRE, WARWICK-SHIRE)

Good beer country, with an abundance of pubs offering the real thing in great variety, especially in the Birmingham-Wolverhampton-Dudley area. This is one of the remaining strongholds of mild. In the Potteries and in the Black Country about three times as much mild is drunk as bitter, always in thin-walled, straight-sided glasses. Such bitter as is brewed tends to be rather sweet and bland, at least to southern tastes. The region is especially fortunate in having no fewer than three of the country's handful of pubs that still brew their own beer. These are:

All Nations Inn, Coalport Road, Madeley, Telford, Shropshire,

where Mrs W. H. Lewis has done all the brewing for the past 40 years, producing a light mild in weekly brews.

The Old Swan Brewery, Halesowen Road, High Street, Netherton, Dudley.

The Pardoe family have been brewing for more than 40 years, supplying beer to the Old Swan and also to the White Swan, Holland Street, Dudley. Over the door of the Old Swan Inn, Netherton, are written the words 'Doris Clare Pardoe, Licensed brewer and retailer of ales' and inside the pub a sign proudly advertises that 'The ALES brewed at this Establishment are the PUREST in the Borough. Brewed by a "Medalist" and Certificated Brewer.' Mrs Pardoe, herself a teetotaller, brews a most enjoyable mildish bitter and sells it at a very reasonable price. With its engraved mirrors, elaborate enamelled ceiling and stove in the middle of the room (in winter radiating an astounding heat) the pub makes a most pleasant place in which to enjoy it.

Three Tuns Brewery, Bishop's Castle, Shropshire

For ninety years the Roberts family brewed outstanding bitter and mild in the imposing nineteenth-century brewhouse at the back of the inn. In 1976 the Three Tuns changed hands.

On a scale not much larger than these is:

Daniel Batham and Sons, Delph Brewery, Brierley Hill, Staffordshire,

which has only eight pubs. One of these stands next to the brewery. It's name is The Vine, but it is generally known

as the The Bull and Bladder, apparently because there used
to be a slaughter-house next door. The brewer's slogan
comes from Shakespeare – 'Blessing of your heart; you
brew good ale' – and the boast is justified. All Batham's
beer is draught, comes in wooden casks and is served by
hand pumps. The bitter is a strong one, and the mild won
first prize in its class at the 1972 Brewex Exhibition.

Other independent breweries in the area are:

Davenports Brewery Ltd, Bath Row, Birmingham
More than 100 pubs concentrating in the Birmingham area
but spreading out to Coventry, Leamington, Warwick,
Worcestershire and as far as Wales. There's also a widespread
club trade, and a most unusual home delivery service.
The tasty bitter and the dark mild are served without
pressure in nearly half of their tied houses.

Holden's Brewery Ltd, Hopden Brewery, Woodsetten, Dudley,
Worcestershire
Nine pubs within a few miles of the brewery selling 'The
Beer with the Glow'. Until recently the mild was the only
draught beer, with the bitter coming in keg form, but the
bitter is now occasionally to be found on hand pumps, and
there is a draught Old Ale at Christmas.

J. P. Simpkiss, Dennis Brewery, Brettell Lane, Brierley Hill,
Staffordshire
Sixteen tied houses in and near Brierley Hill. Draught
bitter, dark mild and (in winter) a dark Old, usually on
hand or electric pumps.

Marston, Thompson and Evershed, The Brewery, Shobnall
Road, Burton-on-Trent, Staffordshire
About 700 pubs over an exceptionally wide area extending
from Wales to Leicester, from Cumbria to London (at
the Cheshire Cheese, just off Fleet Street). There are two
draught bitters – Draught BB and the excellent Pedigree –
and a dark mild. Owd Roger, a barley wine, is generally
available in bottled form: the draught version used to
be found only at the Royal Standard of England, near

Beaconsfield, Bucks but is now in a few other pubs as well. Most Marston's pubs use electric or hand pumps. There's a strong low-calorie bottled beer called Low Cal.

Wolverhampton and Dudley Breweries Ltd has two breweries: *Banks's Park Brewery*, Wolverhampton, and *Julia Hanson and Sons*, High Street and Greystone Street, Dudley

Between them they have some 800 pubs, mostly west of Birmingham in the area between Wolverhampton and Kidderminster. Banks's draught bitter and light mild are usually served without pressure, and there is a very strong bottled barley wine called Old Ale which is over 8 per cent alcohol. Hanson's also has draught bitter and light mild.

There are two local breweries belonging to national companies, both of which have a strong local following. *Ansells*, Aston Brewery, Aston Cross, Birmingham, is part of Allied Breweries. Ansells has 2,000 pubs serving draught bitter, a dark mild and also, particularly in the Potteries, a light mild. *Mitchells and Butlers* is now part of Bass Charrington. Its Cape Hill Brewery in Birmingham is said to be the biggest producer of traditional cask beer in the world.

EAST MIDLANDS (DERBYSHIRE, NOTTINGHAMSHIRE, LINCOLNSHIRE, LEICESTERSHIRE, RUTLAND)

Independent companies in this wide and varied area are:
George Bateman and Son Ltd, Salem Bridge Brewery, Wainfleet, Skegness, Lincolnshire

One hundred and forty pubs all over Lincolnshire, concentrated around Wainfleet, in all of which the draught beer comes direct from the cask by gravity or is pumped without top-pressure. This family firm justifiably boasts its 'Good Honest Ales'. The draught bitter and the light mild are both recommended.

Brewpubs Ltd, 7 Teigh Road, Market Overton, Oakham, Rutland

This company was founded in 1975 by Roger Booth, formerly a brewer for Nimmo's, and inventor of the Tom Caxton home-brew kit. The aim of the company is to start a chain of pubs all brewing their own beer to local requirements, and franchising equipment to other free houses on a royalty basis. The first into operation is the Fighting Cocks, Corby Glen, Grantham, Lincolnshire. It seems a most promising idea, but at the time of writing it is too early to comment further on the project.

Everards Brewery Ltd. 39 Castle St, Leicester

Nearly 130 pubs mostly in and around Leicester, and a handful in Nottingham, though the beer is actually brewed in Burton-on-Trent. Having apparently turned its back on traditional draught beer Everards has now shown signs of returning to the paths of righteousness by producing a powerful traditional cask bitter called Old Original.

Hardys and Hansons, Kimberley Brewery, Kimberley, Nottingham

Two neighbouring breweries that shared a well and after 70 years of competition amalgamated in 1930. More than 200 pubs in the Nottingham-Chesterfield-Derby area. There's a dark mild, and a well-hopped bitter which carried off a top prize at the Brewex 1972 exhibition. The draught beer is usually served without top-pressure.

Home Brewery, The Brewery, Mansfield Road, Daybrook, Nottinghamshire

Some 400 pubs, mostly within 50 miles of Nottingham, but extending throughout the East Midlands from Northampton to Leeds and east to the Lincolnshire coast. The draught bitter and dark mild are usually served by traditional means, and there's a strong bottled beer called Bendigo which is worth a try.

T. Hoskins Ltd, Beaumanor Road, Leicester

The only tied house is the Red Lion, Park Street, Market Bosworth, ten miles from the brewery. However, the slogan is 'Have a drink at home', so take a jug or some empty bottles and fill them up with draught beer at the off-licence next to the brewery. There's bitter and a dark mild. Hoskins's beer is also available in some free houses around Leicester.

Mansfield Brewery Co. Ltd, Littleworth, Mansfield, Nottinghamshire

About 180 pubs. Mansfield used to brew fine beer, but it's all 'bright' and top-pressure now, and the bitter tastes terribly sweet to me.

G. Ruddle and Co., The Brewery, Langham, Oakham, Rutland

Note the address. Rutland is a small county, but makes up in beauty for what it lacks in size. It is important to resist the GPO's foolish pretence that Rutland has ceased to exist. This company produces some of the best beer in the country, and in the past few years its fortunes have been completely reversed by the new-found enthusiasm for real beer. There are nearly 50 tied houses in the immediate area, all tenanted, and a growing free trade in Nottinghamshire, the South Midlands and in and around London. The draught County is a powerful 1050 o.g. which seems too much for me for midday drinking, when I would stick to the excellent ordinary bitter. But they're both outstandingly good. Indeed, I would put Ruddle's beer in the top half-dozen in the country.

James Shipstone and Sons, Star Brewery, New Basford, Nottingham

Shippo's, as it's called in Nottingham (which in Nottingham is pronounced Dottigub) has 250 pubs, mostly in Nottinghamshire, Leicestershire and Derbyshire. It is easy to catch the enthusiasm expressed by locals for the mild and the bitter, both very well-flavoured, and served without top-pressure in nearly all their houses.

SOUTH MIDLANDS (BEDFORDSHIRE, HERTFORD-
SHIRE, HUNTINGDONSHIRE, NORTHAMPTONSHIRE)

Litchborough Brewing Company, Litchborough, Northamptonshire
was started in 1974 by Bill Urquhart who had been made
redundant after being head brewer of Watney's brewery
in Northampton (formerly Phipps). Quantities produced
are fairly small, and unfortunately seem to be somewhat
removed from traditional cask beer.

McMullen and Sons, Old Cross, Hertford
Nearly 200 pubs in central and eastern Hertfordshire and
north-west Essex. Draught bitter and light mild, usually
served under pressure – sometimes carbon dioxide, and
sometimes by air pressure.

Paine and Co., St Neots, Huntingdonshire
Twenty-four tied houses in and around St Neots. Draught
bitter and dark mild, and a new very strong EG bitter.
Having gone over almost entirely to top-pressure Paine's
have recently been busily switching back to traditional
methods.

Rayment's, Furneux Pelham, Buntingford, Hertfordshire
This subsidiary of Greene King's has 25 pubs in the Herts-
Essex area. Draught bitter, and a light and a dark mild
are mostly served by top-pressure but are pleasant none-
theless.

Charles Wells, Bedford, Bedfordshire
About 270 pubs in Bedfordshire and Northamptonshire,
straying into Hertfordshire and as far as Cambridge. A
tasty well-hopped bitter and a dark mild, and a strong
ale at Christmas, dispensed mostly by top-pressure. A strong
(1015 o.g.) draught bitter called Draught Fargo has recently been introduced.

EAST ANGLIA (NORFOLK, SUFFOLK, ESSEX, CAMBRIDGESHIRE)

Watney's iron grip on Norfolk is relieved only slightly by a few independents. Better prospects in Suffolk and Essex, where there are not many brewers, but what they brew is outstanding.

Adnams and Co., Sole Bay Brewery, Southwold, Suffolk

Seventy-one pubs in east Suffolk, with free trade in Norfolk, Essex and Cambridgeshire. The draught bitter is one of the best in the country, in addition to which there is a dark mild, and at Christmas the impressive Tally Ho barley wine. Adnams have long been staunch defenders of traditional beer, and in all their houses the beer is served by gravity or hand pumps.

Elgood and Sons, North Brink Brewery, Wisbech, Cambridgeshire

Some 60 tied houses around Wisbech, and out as far as Peterborough, Spalding (Lincolnshire) and King's Lynn (Norfolk). Dark mild and an excellent bitter, unfortunately served without top-pressure in only about a half of the pubs.

Greene King, Westgate Brewery, Bury St Edmunds, Suffolk

One of the largest independent companies, with a subsidiary brewery at Biggleswade in Bedfordshire, as well as Rayment's in Hertfordshire. There are some 900 tied houses, mostly in East Anglia, some in Hertfordshire and the west Midlands. The draught Abbot ale is one of the strongest in the country (1048·5 o.g.). The ordinary bitter is also excellent, and there are two milds, a light one and a delicious dark mild. Audit Ale barley wine is also notable (1074·4 o.g.). Most Greene King pubs serve the beer by CO_2 top-pressure, in the belief that this is the best chance for the survival of traditional beer. Greene King has a pub in Bury St Edmunds, the Nutshell, which is the smallest in the country.

T. D. Ridley and Sons, Hartford End, Chelmsford, Essex
More than 60 pubs in central and north-west Essex. The
advertising slogan – 'Draught beer from the wood' – is
no more than the truth. The well-flavoured bitter and mild
is all served from wooden casks by gravity or pump.

Tolly Cobbold, Tollemache and Cobbold Breweries Ltd,
Cliff Brewery, Ipswich, Suffolk
About 380 tied houses, mostly in Suffolk and Cambridgeshire. There's a rather ordinary draught bitter, a mild and
(in winter) an Old ale. The draught Cantab Best, though
brewed in Ipswich, is only supplied to a handful of Cambridge pubs, only on top-pressure. The beer is served by
pressure in most of the company's pubs. The bottled beers
used to have a beautiful label bearing an art nouveau steel
engraving of a diaphanously-clad lady, while the bottles
themselves were shaped like Indian clubs or Perrier bottles.
These have been replaced with conventional bottles and
labels that look like those of Watney's, a confusion most
brewers would avoid. Dreadful joke – Question: 'Why is
Ipswich like an old shoe?' Answer: 'Because it's Cobbold
all over.'

SOUTH-WEST (CORNWALL, DEVON, DORSET,
SOMERSET)

This is cider country, and the area as a whole is low in
choice as far as beer is concerned. In the sixteenth century
Andrew Boorde described the ale of Cornwall as 'looking
white and thick as [if] pigs had wrestled in it', but things
are not quite so bad nowadays. Neither Devon nor Somerset
has an independent brewery, and these counties depend
mostly on Courage (formerly George's of Bristol), Whitbread
and Devenish. North Devon is Watney country, and in the
west of Devon there are few pubs, partly because the

Temperance Societies bought up pubs and turned them into unlicensed People's Refreshment Houses, until the brewers bought out the PRHA. Wadworth and Marston's are both available in Bath, and Wadworth's excellent beers are also to be found in Devon and Somerset. Independent breweries in the area are:

J. A. Devenish, Trinity House, Weymouth, Dorset

More than 400 pubs, mostly in Dorset and western Cornwall. There are 56 in Weymouth alone (population 41,000). There are two draught bitters and a dark mild, almost always served by top-pressure. The keg Saxon is one of the weakest beers in the country.

Eldridge Pope, Dorchester Brewery, Dorchester, Dorset

About 200 pubs in Dorset and Somerset, and east into Hampshire and Wiltshire. Two full-flavoured bitters and a strong dark winter ale, which are mostly served by top-pressure, though the flavour survives the process better than most. A new beer called Royal Oak made its appearance in 1975. This is brewed to a recipe dating from 1896, and comes only in wooden casks, with an original gravity of 1048, which makes it one of the strongest draught beers in the country. The bottled range includes the extremely strong Thomas Hardy ale (about 12 per cent alcohol), which is only brewed occasionally (see page 70-1).

Hall and Woodhouse, The Brewery, Blandford Forum, Dorset

About 250 tied houses in Dorset, Somerset, Hampshire and Wiltshire. Two bitters and a dark mild, but this brewery too is very keen on pressurizing.

Miners' Arms, Priddy, Somerset

Undoubtedly the smallest brewery in the country. In spite of the name, the Miners' Arms is not a pub but a restaurant and if you want the beer you must have a meal (a very good meal too – local snails are a speciality). Paul Leyton's Own Ale is a naturally conditioned bottled beer, and very palatable. If you want to visit, make sure to phone first (Priddy 217), not just to book a table but also for instruc-

tions on how to find this inaccessible place, well-concealed
in the Mendips.

J. C. and R. H. Palmer, Old Brewery, West Bay Road,
Bridport, Dorset

About 70 pubs in and around Bridport, with a few further
afield. The stronger of the two draught bitters is much
tastier, but they are both good, though usually on top-
pressure.

Geoffrey Richards, Blue Anchor, Helston, Cornwall

Geoffrey Richards represents the third generation of his
family to brew at the Blue Anchor, which was bought by
his grandfather more than 100 years ago. There are two
very strong Stingo bitters, as well as special strong brews at
Christmas and Easter.

St Austell Brewery, St Austell, Cornwall

One hundred and thirty-five pubs, mostly in south-west
Cornwall. There's a bitter and a dark mild, often (but
not always) sold on top-pressure. The bottled Prince's Ale
is a strong barley wine (1101·4 o.g., 10·5 per cent alcohol).
In 1975 they produced a new strong draught beer called
Hicks's Special.

SOUTH-CENTRAL ENGLAND (GLOUCESTERSHIRE,
OXFORDSHIRE, WILTSHIRE, BERKSHIRE, HAMP-
SHIRE, ISLE OF WIGHT, CHANNEL ISLANDS)

This part of England is very well provided for, with not
only great variety of good beer, but also some of the best
in the country. Even the national brewers seem to be on their
best behaviour in this area, with Watney's producing its
only traditional beer in the south at Usher's brewery in
Trowbridge. Whitbread's has breweries at Cheltenham,
Marlow, Portsmouth and Romsey. Courage houses have
excellent beer from the former Simonds brewery in Reading
which brews the powerful and excellent Director's bitter

and a delicious mild. The area is also rich in independent brewing companies:

J. Arkell and Sons, Kingsdown Brewery, Upper Stratton, Swindon, Wiltshire

More than 60 pubs, mostly in and around Swindon. Two draught bitters but no mild, usually served under pressure. However, in the last year or so Arkell's have been going back to traditional methods, and have converted some pubs back to hand pumps.

W. H. Brakspear and Sons, The Brewery, Henley-on-Thames, Oxfordshire

About 130 pubs, mostly in the Chilterns and along the Thames. Many are outstandingly attractive country pubs, and it is not uncommon for the beer in a Brakspear house to be served straight from a barrel sitting on or behind the bar. Some of them don't even have a bar, and the landlord carries the beer through on a tray from the kitchen or cellar. Brakspear's brew four draught beers: the Old, which is dark and mellow, and is brewed all year; a mild, which is all right; and two bitters – after long and frequent sampling I am still unable to decide which I prefer. Both are very hoppy and utterly delicious. The Special is stronger, but the ordinary has even more flavour. Anyway, they are among the best draught bitters in the country – though it should be said that in some pubs it's not invariably well-kept. Incidentally, the pubs do not bear the name Brakspear, but the words Henley Brewery on a dark blue board. As well as making this excellent beer the Brakspear family produced the only English pope, Nicolas Brakspear, who became Adrian IV, 1154–59. They founded the brewery more recently, in 1799.

Burt and Co., High Street, Ventnor, Isle of Wight

A small company with only 11 tied houses, mostly in the south-east of the island, but also with a free trade in hotels, clubs and holiday camps. There are two draught bitters and a dark mild, usually on top-pressure.

Donnington Brewery (L. C. Arkell), Stow-on-the-Wold, Gloucestershire

Not the biggest brewery in the country but, with its water-fowl and mill-pond and trout-stream, probably the pret-tiest. There are 17 tied houses in the Cotswolds. Short delivery runs and low transport costs contribute to the firm's profitability, as do such other small-scale (60 barrels a week) advantages as absence of industrial disputes, short chain-of-command and face-to-face personal relation-ships. Two bitters and a dark mild are brewed, and are served without top-pressure in a good many of the pubs, including the Shakespeare, Stratford-on-Avon, and the Queen's Head, Stow-on-the-Wold.

George Gale and Co. Ltd, The Brewery, Horndean, Portsmouth, Hampshire

Most of the tied houses are in Hampshire. No fewer than five draught beers are brewed – all of them good. Horndean Special bitter is one of the strongest draught beers in the country and as well as another bitter, there's a light mild, a dark mild and an Old ale in winter. Hard to obtain, but worth the effort, is the bottled Gale's Prize Old Ale. This is distinguished in four ways – by its reddish colour, by the fact that it is naturally conditioned in cask and bottle for over a year, and comes in a corked bottle, and by its strength (1095 o.g., 10 per cent alcohol).

Gibbs, Mew and Co., Anchor Brewery, Salisbury

Some 50 pubs, mostly around Salisbury. Having produced nothing but keg beer for years, in 1976 they brought out a strong, traditional draught called Bishop's Tipple which is a justification of their slogan 'Gibbus Gibbs Great Beer'.

Hook Norton Brewery Co., Hook Norton, near Banbury, Oxfordshire

Thirty-four tied houses, mostly in the Cotswolds. The brew-ery is a most attractive building in a quiet village, its power coming from a steam-driven piston engine with an eight-foot flywheel, built in 1900. The well-water is so pure that it can be used for brewing without being treated. The draught bitter and mild (Hookey) are both very well-flavoured, and are usually served by hand-pumps. The bottled bitter and mild are much less fizzy than most bottled beers.

Mason Arms, South Liegh, Witney, Oxfordshire
See pages 103-4.

Morland and Co., Ltd, The Brewery, Abingdon, Oxfordshire
The 240 tied houses, almost all in Berkshire and Oxfordshire, include some of the most attractive pubs in the country. The brewery's emblem shows an eighteenth-century painter with a palette on his arm and brush in hand, and George Morland is claimed as a vague relation of the brewing family. The country pubs and alehouses that Morland painted in the eighteenth century are preserved virtually intact in some of the Morland's pubs of today, with their open fireplaces, matchboarding, plain wooden tables and benches, and hooks in the ceiling from which to hang hams. The beer is good. There are two well-flavoured bitters, – the best bitter is to some tastes sometimes too bitter. There's also a good dark mild. Top-pressure in many pubs.

Morrell's, The Lion Brewery, St Thomas Street, Oxford
One hundred and forty pubs, almost all in Oxfordshire. Neither the bitter nor the mild really lives up to the slogan 'The beer with the strength of a lion' but the draught College ale is a strong beer that you won't forget in a hurry. This brewery too has some very pleasant pubs.

Wadworth & Co., Northgate Brewery, Devizes, Wiltshire
Nearly 150 tied houses throughout Wiltshire and out into Gloucestershire, Oxfordshire, Hampshire, Dorset and Somerset, as well as an extensive free trade. There are no fewer than five draught beers: PA (pale ale), IPA (India Pale Ale), 6X, Old Timer and a dark mild. The first three have a distinctive, rather curious but certainly distinctive flavour which to me tastes like caramel. Many people

like it very much. My favourite is the draught Old Timer
which used to be one of the things that reconciled me to
winter until they started brewing it all year. It's very strong:
half-pints recommended. Wadworth's are going for tradi-
tionalism in a big way. The few houses that used top-
pressure are being converted to traditional means of dispense, and the brewery is building up a stable of dray-
horses for delivering beer within Devizes.

THE CHANNEL ISLANDS

Beer in the Channel Islands tends to be stronger and cheaper
than on the mainland, and the licensing hours are extremely
liberal. The four breweries are:

Ann Street, St Helier, Jersey
About 50 pubs in Jersey selling two keg bitters but no real
draught. The States of Jersey has a substantial shareholding,
and gives its dividends to charity.

Guernsey Brewery, South Esplanade, St Peter Port, Guernsey
About 50 pubs, with a free trade in Alderney, Herm and
Sark. The only draught beer is a dry-hopped dark mild,
served without pressure.

Randalls Brewery, Clare Street, St Helier, Jersey
Some 30 houses, as well as free trade on the island. Keg
beer only. I haven't tried it, but Frank Baillie says it has
the characteristics of traditional draught beer.

R. W. Randall, Vauxlaurens Brewery, St Julian's Avenue,
St Peter Port, Guernsey
Seventeen tied houses, as well as free trade in Alderney,
Sark and Guernsey. The well-hopped dark mild is available
on hand pumps.

LONDON

Bass Charrington still have quite a lot of London pubs with
hand pumps but Charrington's bitter is not up to much
nowadays, and only the draught Bass (or Worthington –
they're the same thing, but very much not to be confused
with keg Worthington E) is of interest. Watney's are trying
out real beer, and Courage's seem to be responding to the
demand for real beer, but in truth London would be badly
off without its two independent brewers:
Fuller, Smith and Turner, The Griffin Brewery, Chiswick,
London W4
About 110 pubs, mostly in west London, some in south
London. The Star Tavern in Belgrave Mews West is the
closest to central London, but Fuller's is also available at
the Coronet Bar in Soho Street, off Oxford Street.
The draught bitters – London Pride and Extra
Special Bitter – are both excellent, the latter being probably
the strongest draught beer in Britain (1055·8 o.g.). Fuller's
have in the past favoured a device called the Porter-
Lancastrian system which moves the beer by compressed
air with a light covering of CO_2, but they are now switching some pubs back to hand pumps. The slogan's pun is for
once justified: 'Beer with the Fuller Flavour.'
Young and Co., Ram Brewery, Wandsworth, London SW18
One hundred and forty tied houses, mainly in south-west
London and suburbs, but extending down through Surrey
and Sussex. Committedly traditional, and leaders in pushing
real beer in London. Outstandingly good bitter and Special
bitter, and a strong Winter Warmer (1055 o.g., 5·5 per cent
alcohol). The mild is rather disappointing, but nobody's
perfect. Served without pressure in all pubs.

SOUTH-EAST (KENT, SURREY, SUSSEX)

The independent brewers of this area make up in quality
for what they lack in numbers. There are some black
spots like Brighton, where it's Watney's Watney's everywhere
and never a drop to drink, but otherwise the situation is
fairly pleasant thanks to:
Harvey and Son, Bridge Wharf Brewery, Lewes, Sussex
With its associate, Beard, Harvey's has about 50 tied
houses in east Sussex and going into Kent. Excellent beer.
Two bitters, a dry dark mild, an Old and (mostly in
winter) Elizabethan barley wine. Most pubs serve the beer
without pressure.
King and Barnes, 18 Bishopric, Horsham, Sussex
Fifty-eight tied houses, mostly in west Sussex, but extending
into Surrey. The bitter is not especially strong, but it is
delicious. There's also a dark mild and an Old. Mostly
hand pumped in the pubs.
Shepherd Neame, Faversham Brewery, 17 Court Street,
Faversham, Kent
More than 200 tied houses in Kent and reaching into the
London suburbs. The ordinary bitter is exceptionally
hoppy, and there's a slightly stronger best bitter in some
pubs. There's also a mild and the strong Old English
Stock Ale. Most of the pubs have, and use, hand pumps.
The brewery grows all its own hops on its own farm,
and very nice they taste too.

Wales

The licensing laws in Wales are most peculiar. Pubs often
stay open till 3 p.m., 3.30 or even 4 p.m., and in many
towns the pubs are open all day on market days and bank
holidays. In Carmarthen, for example, there are pubs
which are open all day every Monday, Wednesday,

Thursday, Saturday and the first Friday in the month.
On the other hand there are still areas that are dry on
Sundays.

Independent breweries in Wales are:

Border Breweries, Wrexham, Clwyd

Two hundred pubs serving Wrexham, Oswestry, Shrewsbury, the Anglo-Welsh border, north Wales, and into
England as far as the Potteries. The bitter is reddish in
colour, pleasant in flavour but rather thin. There are also
two milds. The beer is mostly sold without top-pressure.
Ghastly punning slogan: 'Prince of Ales'.

S. A. Brain and Co., The Old Brewery, St Mary Street,
Cardiff

More than 100 pubs in the Cardiff area and west to Swan-
sea. Two distinctive draught bitters and a dark beer called
Red Dragon, served by traditional means in all their
pubs.

Buckley's, The Brewery, Gilbert Road, Llanelli, Dyfed

About 110 pubs in Llanelli, north to Carmarthen, Amman-
ford and Cardigan, and west to Pembroke, and a few in
other parts of Wales. Two well-hopped bitters and a dark
mild, usually served without top-pressure.

Felinfoel Brewery Co., Felinfoel Brewery, Llanelli, Dyfed

Nearly 80 pubs in Llanelli and the counties of Carmarthen,
Pembroke and Cardigan. Two bitters and a darkish mild,
usually served by top-pressure.

Miskin Arms, Miskin, Pontyclun, Glamorgan

A free house which started brewing its own beer in 1976.

South Wales and Monmouthshire United Clubs' Brewery, Pontyclun, Glamorganshire

One of the two remaining club breweries (see Northern
Clubs' Federation Brewery, page 185). Supplies 350
clubs in South Wales and some parts of England. Two
draught bitters, very good, sometimes served by top-
pressure but not always.

Scotland

Scotland presents a rather gloomy prospect for the beer enthusiast. The country has fallen to keg, lager, top-pressure and very cold beer. Relief is provided by:

The Belhaven Brewery, Dunbar, East Lothian

Scotland's oldest independent brewery. Excellent draught Export, Heavy and Light. Hand pumped at the Old Howgate Inn, Penicuik, Midlothian, and on the vernacular water-pump at the Golf Inn, Bishopton, Renfrewshire.

Maclay and Co., Thistle Brewery, Alloa, Clackmannanshire

About 30 tied houses, mostly in central Scotland. Three well-hopped draught bitters, mostly pressurized.

Traquair House, Innerleithen, Peeblesshire

A twelfth-century house where brewing recommenced in a restored brewhouse in 1965 after an interruption of 200 years. There are three or four brews a year producing a beer of 1080 o.g. for bottling. Each bottle is numbered, and the contents are marvellous. Traquair House is open to the public in the summer, and the beer is also available (at a price) in hotels and inns in Edinburgh and southern Scotland.

Ushers, Ushers Brewery Ltd, The Park Brewery, Edinburgh

A subsidiary of Vaux, with 200 pubs throughout Scotland, mostly in Edinburgh. No real beer, but some have found the Dark Heavy palatable.

Isle of Man

The high quality of the beer on the island is maintained by the Manx Pure Beer Act, which permits the use only of hops, malt and sugar in brewing. Furthermore top-pressure seems to be almost unknown to the fortunate Manxmen. The two local breweries are:

Castletown Brewery, Victoria Road, Castletown

Thirty six pubs, selling the rather similar draught mild and bitter.
Okell and Son, Falcon Brewery, Douglas
Seventy pubs. The draught mild and bitter are both pleasant.

Ireland

Ireland means stout, and stout means Guinness. The Guinness Company commands more than 90 per cent of the beer market in the Republic, and very nearly as much in Northern Ireland. The proportion of bottled Guinness to draught is about one to three. In recent years there has been a great increase in the popularity of Smithwick's ale, a mildish bitter brewed in Kilkenny in a brewery belonging to, of course, Guinness. In fact Guinness are not the only brewers in Ireland. As always, Cork has to be different and has Beamish and Crawford, which brews a sweetish stout as well as Bass and Carling, and Murphy's which brews an excellent stout, rather similar to Guinness, as well as Schooner ale. Northern Ireland is showing an increasing partiality to lager, but to be serious for a moment, if you're going to Ireland you really should drink Guinness.

Select Bibliography

Frank Baillie: *The Beer Drinker's Companion.* David and
  Charles, 1975
Alfred Barnard: *The Noted Breweries of Great Britain and
  Ireland.* 3 volumes. Sir Joseph Causton and Sons, 1889
Tom Barrett: *Darts.* Pan, 1973
Denzil Batchelor: *The English Inn.* Batsford, 1963
John Bickerdyke: *The Curiosities of Ale and Beer.* Field and
  Tuer, 1886
Andrew Boorde: *Compendious Regyment on Dyetary of
  Health*, London, 1542
Michael Brander: *The Life and Sport of the Inn.* Gentry
  Books, 1973
Brewers' Society Statistical Handbook. Brewing Publications,
  1975
Thomas Burke: *English Inns.* Collins, 1944
William Cobbett: *Cottage Economy*, 1821
H. S. Corran: *A History of Brewing.* David and Charles,
  1975
T. E. B. Clarke: *What's Yours?* Peter Davies, 1938
Elizabeth David: *Spices, Salt and Aromatics in the English
  Kitchen.* Penguin, 1970
J. C. Drummond and Anne Wilbraham: *The Englishman's
  Food.* Cape, Revised edition, 1957
Lord Erroll of Hale (chairman): Report of the Depart-
  mental Committee on Liquor Licensing. Cmnd.5154.
  HMSO, 1972
Evening Standard Guide to London Pubs. Pan, 1973
Carole Fahy: *Cooking with Beer.* Elm Tree Books, 1972
Timothy Finn: *The Watney Book of Pub Games.* Queen
  Anne Press, 1966

Pub Games of England. Queen Anne Press, 1975

J. K. Galbraith: *The New Industrial State*. Penguin Books, 1968

Mark Girouard: *Victorian Pubs*. Studio Vista, 1975

The Good Beer Guide. Arrow Books for the Campaign for Real Ale, 1976

Maurice Gorham and H. McG. Dunnett: *Inside the Pub*. Architectural Press, 1950

Martin Green and Tony White: *Guide to London Pubs*. Sphere Books, 1968

Graham Greene: *A Sort of Life*. Penguin Books, 1974

Geoffrey Grigson: *The Englishman's Flora*. Phoenix House, 1958; Paladin, 1975

Jane Grigson: *Good Things*. Michael Joseph, 1971

Frederick W. Hackwood: *Inns, Ales, and Drinking Customs of Old England*. T. Fisher Unwin, 1909

Brian Harrison: *Drink and the Victorians: the temperance question in England 1815–1872*. Faber and Faber, 1971

Louis Heren: *Growing Up Poor in London*. Hamish Hamilton, 1973

Christopher Hutt: *The Death of the English Pub*. Arrow Books, Hutchinson, 1973

Hurford Janes: *The Red Barrel: a history of Watney Mann*. John Murray, 1963

Frank A. King: *Beer has a History*. Hutchinson, 1947

James Lightbody: *Every Man His Own Gauger*. Hugh Newman, at the Grasshopper, next the Rose Tavern in the Poultrey, 1695

Norman Longmate: *The Waterdrinkers*. Hamish Hamilton, 1968

John Mark: *The British Brewing Industry*. Lloyds Bank Review, April 1974

Peter Mathias: *The Brewing Industry in England 1700–1830*. Cambridge, 1959

Mass Observation: *The Pub and the People*. Gollancz, 1943

Angus McGill (editor): *Pub*. Longmans, 1969

H. A. Monckton: *A History of the English Public House*.
Bodley Head, 1969
A History of English Ale and Beer. Bodley Head, 1966
The Monopolies Commission: *Beer: a report on the supply
of beer*. HMSO, 1969
George Orwell: *A Clergyman's Daughter*. Penguin Books, 1969
John Piper: *Buildings and Prospects*. Architectural Press,
1948
C. F. Pratten: *Economies of Scale in Manufacturing Industry*.
Occasional Paper no 28. Department of Applied
Economics, Cambridge
Philippa Pullar: *Consuming Passions*. Hamish Hamilton,
1970
Timothy M. Richards and James Stevens Curl: *City of
London Pubs*. David and Charles, 1973
E. F. Schumacher: *Small is Beautiful*. Blond and Briggs,
1973
John Skelton: *Poems*, edited by Robert S. Kinsman.
Oxford, Clarendon Press, 1969
Johnny Speight: *It Stands to Reason*. Michael Joseph, 1973
Brian Spicer: *The Story of Beer*. Geographical Magazine
vol. 28, 1955
Brian Spiller: *Victorian Public Houses*. David and Charles,
1972
Reay Tannahill: *Food in History*. Eyre Methuen, 1973
W. H. T. Tayleur: *The Penguin Book of Home-Brewing and
Wine-Making*. Penguin, 1973
Arthur R. Taylor: *Pleasure at the Pub: an introduction to
English Pub Games*. Mayflower, 1976
G. M. Trevelyan: *English Social History*. Penguin Books
John Vaizey: *The Brewing Industry 1886–1951: an economic
study*. Pitman, 1960
Colin Wilson: *A Book of Booze*. Gollancz, 1974
The Story of Whitbread's. Whitbread & Co (3rd edition),
1964
C. Anne Wilson: *Food and Drink in Britain*. Constable, 1973

Index

Index

A Fontana Selection

The Sunday Gardener *(illus.)*, edited by Alan Gemmell
Ideology in Social Science, edited by Robin Blackburn
Hitler: The Führer and the People, J. P. Stern
Memories, Dreams, Reflections, C. G. Jung
The Screwtape Letters, C. S. Lewis
Waiting on God, Simone Weil
Butterflies *(illus.)*, E. B. Ford
Marx, David McLellan
Soft City, Jonathan Raban
Social Welfare in Modern Britain, edited by Butterworth & Holman
Europe: Hierarchy and Revolt 1320-1450, George Holmes
Black Holes, John Taylor
The First Four Georges *(illus.)*, J. H. Plumb
Letters of Vincent Van Gogh *(illus.)*, edited by Mark Roskill
Food for Free *(illus.)*, Richard Mabey
Language Made Plain, Anthony Burgess

Into Unknown England 1866-1913

Selections from the Social Explorers

Edited by Peter Keating

How did the poor live in late Victorian and Edwardian England? In the slums of London and Birmingham? In the iron-town of Middlesbrough? In a Devon fishing village? In rural Essex?

This is a fascinating sequence of extracts from the writings of those individuals, journalists and wealthy businessmen, a minister's wife, and a popular novelist, who temporarily left the comfort of their middle-class homes to find out how the other half lived. Peter Keating includes material from Charles Booth, Jack London, B. S. Rowntree and C. F. G. Masterman as well as by such lesser-known figures as George Sims, Andrew Mearns and Stephen Reynolds.

'. . . a brilliant and compelling anthology . . . *Into Unknown England* is not only an education in itself, throwing into three-dimensional chiaroscuro the flat statistics of "scientific" history, but a splendid example of prose which is always immediate and alive.'
Alan Brien, *Spectator*

'The writers collected here used all the techniques they could to solicit sympathy. Their descendants are a thousand television documentaries.'
Paul Barker, *The Times*

'. . . a rich collection of passages, intelligently presented.'
Guardian

Keywords
Raymond Williams

Alienation, creative, family, media, radical, structural, taste: these are seven of the hundred or so words whose derivation, development and contemporary meaning Raymond Williams explores in this unique study of the language in which we discuss 'culture' and 'Society'.

A series of connecting essays investigating how these 'keywords' have been formed, redefined, confused and reinforced as the historical contexts in which they were applied changed to give us their current meaning and significance.

'This is a book which everyone who is still capable of being educated should read.'   Christopher Hill, *New Society*

'. . . for the first time we have some of the materials for constructing a genuinely historical and a genuinely social semantics . . . Williams's book is unique in its kind so far and it provides a model as well as a resource for us all.'
Alasdair MacIntyre, *New Statesman*

'. . . an important book.'   F. W. Bateson, *Guardian*

'. . . excellent and penetrating. It must be added to any shelf of reference books about words.'   Woodrow Wyatt, *Sunday Times*